ONE PAGE AT A TIME

This book is a work of non-fiction. All exercises have been curated and compiled by the author and in some cases reformatted or reworked to embody the Wondershift way.

ISBN: 979-8-9882755-3-4

Front cover and content designed by Judy Goldberg & Madeline Arnoldy

First printing edition of the Leader Edition

www.wondershift.biz

WONDERSHIFT

This journal belongs to...

WONDERSHIFT

Foreword

Success in today's world requires you to be at your best — not just to inspire your team, but to collaborate effectively with peers and engage meaningfully with customers. Life is already complex. "Wake Up and Wondershift Leader Edition" provides a personalized, step-by-step approach, allowing you to choose where to begin as you elevate your leadership.

Being a leader today may be quite different from when you started your first job. We've witnessed rapid technological advances, shifts in political and economic landscapes, and a global pandemic that reshaped the way we live and work. With multiple generations in the workforce, the dynamics of leadership continue to evolve.

Innovation, efficiency, and a competitive edge are essential in today's fast-paced environment. The ability to empower people to perform at their highest level has never been more critical, and it all starts with strong leadership.

The way we connect and collaborate is being redefined. The pursuit of opportunity will require you to think differently and break the rules that paralyze change. Judy Goldberg invites you to turn these insights into action.

Kirstin Furber

Kirstin Furber
Chief People Officer and Media Executive

Dear Leader,

Every day, you make hundreds of decisions large and small that shape outcomes, and more importantly, the lives of your employees. Drawing from 30+ years experience working with global leaders, I've witnessed firsthand the double edged sword of leadership. While effective leadership nurtures growth and trustworthiness, challenged leadership jeopardizes the results talented people deliver. In fact, research shows that poor leadership negatively impacts the bottom line by reducing productivity, stifling innovation, and causing significant financial losses. This is your invitation to elevate your leadership, team success, and organizational impact.

Together, we'll consider ...

- How the decisions you make today shape the culture your people experience tomorrow
- The stories your employees tell about working with you
- The leadership legacy you are creating, intentionally or unintentionally
- The behavioral patterns and blind spots you might need to address
- The ways in which you could better align your leadership impact with your deepest values

This journal is your guide. Whether you engage with it alone, with a colleague, or with your team, it's designed to help you connect with your purpose, refine your approach, and lead with greater intention. The way you show up each day has a ripple effect, impacting performance metrics and the very well-being, confidence, success, and engagement of those who look to you for guidance.

Driven to explore the psychological and emotional effects of leadership on employees, I launched a personal research project. I gathered data through surveys and personal interviews by asking employees to describe their experiences of working with both 'desirable' and 'undesirable' leadership. This surfaced the gap between leaders who inspire and uplift and leaders who create environments of fear, burnout and disengagement.

The survey spanned six continents, 36 countries, and 20 industries, gathering responses from 430 people, ages 18 to 74, across multiple sectors including Aerospace, Education, Health Care, Manufacturing, and Media. Wondershift explored the impact of great leadership and focused on how negative behaviors affect employees' well-being, resilience, and long-term success.

One truth clearly emerged: leadership is never neutral.

At Wondershift, we know how important it is for leaders like you to have practical tools for growth at your fingertips. That's why we created "Wake Up and Wondershift Leader Edition".

Imagine starting each day not just leading, but fully aligned with your values, intentional in your actions, and deeply connected to those you serve. These pages will help you do just that, allowing you to build a leadership legacy that stands the test of time.

Your journey begins here. Where it leads is up to you.

Judy Goldberg

Founder, Wondershift LLC

WONDERSHIFT

Wondershift Study Findings

Here are a few key insights that stood out for how desirable and undesirable leadership behaviors impact trust, engagement, performance, and health.

The three most consistently referenced UNDESIRABLE traits of a leader were...

MICRO-MANAGER
SELFISH
BULLY

The three most consistently referenced DESIRABLE traits of a leader were...

EMPOWERING
SUPPORTIVE
EMPATHETIC

THE IMPACT OF AN UNDESIRABLE LEADER

60%
ARE ON EDGE
CONSISTENTLY

"Despite enjoying the role, my mental and physical health declined, I lost confidence and motivation and eventually sought out other employment."
-Jamie

THE POSITIVE BENEFITS OF A DESIRABLE LEADER

85% **SAID**
THE LEADER CHANGED
THEIR LIFE

"At one of our first meetings, she asked me what I most loved to do at work and from then on gave me every opportunity she could to let me work on that skill." - Anonymous

What shocked us the most...

Three specific and quite alarming behaviors described by a few of our survey respondents said their manager was...

CREEPY **BLOOD-THIRSTY** **DOUCHEY**

Specific phrases undesirable leaders used:

"You need to do what I say, and NO is not an option."

"Listen to me!"

"Do you know who I am?"

"Never lie to me, never try and keep anything from me, and never talk about me."

"There IS one right way, and that IS MY way!"

The very real impact of an undesirable leader:

17% of employees submitted their resignation or left their jobs on the spot

12% of employees took sick leave, entered the hospital, and continue to deal with anxiety and other mental and emotional issues today

15% of employees avoided, retreated, withdrew, hid, or kept their head down to feel safe

CONTACT US TO LEARN MORE ABOUT WONDERSHIFT'S STUDY FINDINGS

WONDERSHIFT

ABCs of Leadership

Based on the Wondershift study, this A-Z list highlights the most desirable behaviors, traits, and characteristics of leaders.

- **A** Approach leadership with a no ego, down-to-earth attitude; be a human first
- **B** Believe in others more than they might believe in themselves
- **C** Create a culture where new ideas are welcomed and considered
- **D** Demonstrate the company values you expect in both words and actions
- **E** Encourage personal and professional growth opportunities and challenges
- **F** Focus on clear communication when sharing the vision and goals
- **G** Give credit generously and recognize the contributions of others
- **H** Handle disagreements constructively and accept dissent when it arises
- **I** Invest time in building trust, fostering relationships, and ensuring team cohesion
- **J** Judge situations fairly and without bias to build trust
- **K** Keep learning about yourself, your team, your customer, the business, the industry
- **L** Lead with empathy by supporting challenges and celebrating successes
- **M** Match your actions with your words so there's no confusion within the team
- **N** Notice when someone has not had a chance to speak and invite them in
- **O** Own your decisions and tackle tough conversations
- **P** Promote psychological safety to empower risk-taking and innovation
- **Q** Question your assumptions and be open to changing your view
- **R** Recognize the value of listening to ideas, feedback, and concerns
- **S** Share your knowledge willingly and enthusiastically with others
- **T** Take action swiftly when you need to apologize or correct a mistake
- **U** Understand the details and dive into nuances when necessary
- **V** Vary the way you communicate to get the best out of each person
- **W** Work through tough decisions with compassion and care for those affected
- **X** X-cel at follow-through by analyzing outcomes and reflecting on lessons
- **Y** Yield to the expertise of your colleagues and team
- **Z** Zoom out regularly to ensure decisions align with the bigger picture

WONDERSHIFT

Why are journaling and self-reflection key practices for great leaders?

BUILDS AWARENESS

Self-reflection enables leaders to become aware of their individual strengths and weaknesses. It also enables them to capitalize on strengths and work to improve on weaknesses.

Source: Lanaj, K., Foulk, T. A., & Jennings, R. E. (2023). Improving the lives of leaders: The beneficial effects of positive leader self-reflection. Journal of Management.

STRENGTHENS ADAPTABILITY

The practice of self-reflection allows leaders to gain insights that empower them to adapt to new situations and information.

Source: Lanaj, K., Foulk, T. A., & Jennings, R. E. (2023). Improving the lives of leaders: The beneficial effects of positive leader self-reflection. Journal of Management.

ENABLES YOUR TEAM

Modeling self-reflection encourages your team members to adopt reflective mentalities as well.

Source: Esther Han (2023),The Importance of Reflective Leadership in Business. Harvard Business School Online.

OFFERS NEW DATA POINTS

Leaders who utilize reflection gain additional data points through the consideration of their own knowledge and insight as they make decisions.

Source: Chiarelli, Christy. 2024. "The Use of Reflection As an Effective Leadership Practice: An Introduction: AEC811 WC473, 9 2024". EDIS 2024 (5). Gainesville, FL.

IMPROVES EMPATHY

Pausing to examine a situation from multiple perspectives allows leaders to demonstrate increased empathy, thus increasing the likelihood of improved connections with others.

Source: Chiarelli, Christy. 2024. "The Use of Reflection As an Effective Leadership Practice: An Introduction: AEC811 WC473, 9 2024". EDIS 2024 (5). Gainesville, FL.

ENHANCES MORALITY

Research shows that deliberate reflection enhances moral consciousness, ethical decision making, and moral leadership.

Source: Branson, 2007; Thiel, Bagdasarov, Harkrider, Johnson, & Mumford, 2012.

Using this Journal

A TOPLINE GUIDE

1 Orient yourself to the Layers of Leadership on the next page and capture the change you'd like to make for each: leading self, leading others, and leading an organization.

2 Explore each chapter

Scan Yourself: Examine core values, leadership behaviors and patterns, uncover limiting beliefs, and craft guiding principles to anchor your personal approach to leadership.

Harness Your Integrity: Clarify decision-making, determine which boundaries to establish or release, identify feedback to act upon, and practice intentionality.

Invest Your Time: Concentrate on where energy, time and money is allocated, learn to set priorities for yourself and your team, and prioritize self-care to align with values.

Foster Community: Build and nurture meaningful relationships, promote inclusivity, and examine the roles necessary to meet the collective needs of multiple audiences.

Tend to the Bigger Picture: Navigate higher-level focus, evaluate what works, what doesn't, and use decision-making frameworks to make informed choices.

3 Examine the elements of each chapter

- A Cover Page to introduce the theme.
- An Overview of the chapter and a list of exercises and writing prompts.
- Exercises with directions. Each exercise may vary in the time it takes to complete.
- Writing Prompts to collect your thoughts, explore the future, and identify patterns.
- Chapter Reflections to capture thoughts, feelings, movements, and insights.

4 Choose your own adventure depending on your desired leadership shift

- Go in order: Start at the beginning and move through each page to the end.
- Select at random: Pick a chapter that grabs your attention and dive in.
- Connect with a colleague: Pick a page that you both complete and then discuss.

5 Take Note

- A Moment for Reflection: Offers space to capture thoughts and progress on your goals.
- Sources & References: Listed by page number based on content provided.

6 Define your definition of 'done' so that you can measure your growth and celebrate the milestones that matter most to you.

- For some, 'done' may be completing all the exercises, taking action, or achieving a shift.
- For others, it might mean finishing one chapter and reflecting on it with their teams.

Layers of Leadership

HOW LEADERS PROGRESS

This journal highlights three layers of leadership to move you through a journey to elevate your impact and influence. Each layer builds on the previous one, starting with self-leadership, then expanding to lead others, and finally influencing larger systems. This progression facilitates personal success and broader business growth.

Leading Self

Leading starts with self-examination, which builds self-awareness and allows you to identify strengths and areas for growth. It aligns your actions with your core values, making your leadership more authentic. By reflecting on your biases, you can improve decision-making and set the foundation for leading others with integrity and intention.

ALIGNS WITH CHAPTERS...

- S Scan Yourself
- H Harness Your Integrity

Leading Others

Once you've cultivated self-awareness, you can more effectively lead others. Leading from your values will build trust, foster collaboration and create an environment where people feel valued and motivated. With a shared purpose, you can guide your team and colleagues to create a supportive space where people will grow and thrive as individuals and collectively.

ALIGNS WITH CHAPTERS...

- H Harness Your Integrity
- I Invest Your Time
- F Foster Community

Leading an Organization

With a strong foundation in leading yourself and others, you're well-equipped to steer an entire organization. As a leader, your role is to consistently articulate the company vision, to navigate challenges, drive innovation, and ensure financial accountability, while fostering a culture that develops and empowers your people, and delivers results.

ALIGNS WITH CHAPTERS...

- F Foster Community
- T Tend to the Bigger Picture

Setting Intentions

As a leader, nothing is static. Leadership requires continuous growth and adaptation at every level, whether you're leading yourself, others, or an organization. Use this space to define your intentions and the meaningful impact you aspire to make at each level of leadership.

My Leadership SHIFT:

Note: Start with a verb to encourage an active and proactive mindset.

When it comes to Leading Self I would like to...

When it comes to Leading Others I would like to...

When it comes to Leading an Organization I would like to...

Chapters

Each chapter offers targeted exercises, writing prompts, and self-assessment tools designed to guide you through a deep introspective process. This will enable you to adapt effectively to changing circumstances while cultivating a leadership style that is both authentic and aligned with your core values and objectives.

S

Scan Yourself

Examine your core values, leadership behaviors and patterns, uncover limiting beliefs, and craft guiding principles to anchor your personal approach to leadership.

H

Harness Your Integrity

Clarify your decision-making frameworks, determine which boundaries to establish or release, identify feedback to act upon, and practice intentionality in your words and actions.

I

Invest Your Time

Concentrate on where your energy, time and money is allocated, learn to set priorities for yourself and your team, and prioritize self-care to align with your values.

F

Foster Community

Build and nurture meaningful relationships, take on roles necessary to meet the collective needs of multiple audiences, and promote a more inclusive culture and community.

T

Tend To The Bigger Picture

Navigate higher level focus by balancing strategic vision with attention to detail. Evaluate what works, what doesn't, and use decision-making frameworks to make informed choices.

Table of Contents

*Writing Prompts in Gray

Scan Yourself

Words of Wonder

“Knowing yourself is the beginning of all wisdom.”
– Aristotle

“Watch your thoughts, for they become words.
Watch your words, for they become actions.
Watch your actions, for they become habits.
Watch your habits, for they become your character.
And watch your character, for it becomes your destiny!”
– Unknown

“Introspection invites us to reassess, realign, and emerge with clarity and strength from within.”
– Judy Goldberg

Scan Yourself

What does this chapter cover?

Examine your core values, leadership behaviors and patterns, uncover limiting beliefs, and craft guiding principles to anchor your personal approach to leadership.

Why does this matter?

In her book, "Insight", Tasha Eurich argues that self-awareness is the 'meta-skill of the 21st Century.' However, she found only 10% to 15% of people are self-aware. Great leadership starts with digging deep into who you are and how others perceive you so you can tweak your leadership accordingly to ensure effectiveness.

What will you gain?

Deepening your self-awareness as a leader builds a solid foundation, empowering you to lead with authenticity and unwavering confidence.

EXERCISES

- The Leader I Want to Be
- Personal SWOT
- Defining Your Values
- User Manual
- Limiting Beliefs
- Know-Do-Be
- Avoidance Behaviors Defined
- Avoidance Behavior Bingo
- Avoiding Avoidance Behaviors
- Story of Your Name
- Recognizing Stress Cues

WRITING PROMPTS

- Growth Behaviors
- Three Core Values
- Energy Tracker
- Blind Spot
- Emotion Map
- Joy List

GROWTH BEHAVIORS: What behaviors are supporting your growth, what's getting in your way, and what new practice could elevate your leadership?

Date:

The Leader I Want to Be

Reflect on your leadership journey by identifying pivotal moments that have shaped your approach. Envision the specific leadership qualities you want to develop and strengthen so you can lead at your best, delivering impact for your team, stakeholders, and community as you build your path forward.

As a leader, I want to be remembered for...

To best support my team, I focus on...

When reflecting on my impact, I notice that I...

A specific moment that challenged my leadership and taught me something valuable was...

One way I will ensure my leadership aligns with my values is by...

Personal SWOT

Use the questions and examples to reflect on your key leadership skills and traits. Conduct your personal leadership SWOT on the next page.

STRENGTHS

Internal factors that you do well as a leader that set you apart from others.

ASK YOURSELF:

- What feedback have I received from peers, supervisors, or my team about what I do well?
- What tasks do I handle with confidence and ease?
- What leadership qualities set me apart?
- In what areas do I consistently excel?

EXAMPLES:

- I actively listen and check for understanding.
- I use data to make sound decisions.
- I defuse high-tension situations effectively.

WEAKNESSES

Internal challenges or areas for improvement as a leader.

ASK YOURSELF:

- Where do I feel less confident as a leader?
- In what areas do I need development?
- What feedback or recurring challenges come up for me as a leader?
- Where have I received constructive criticism?

EXAMPLES:

- I can be overly methodical, taking too long to act when I need to.
- I show my stress in times of uncertainty.
- I don't keep up with the latest trends.

OPPORTUNITIES

External factors that can be leveraged to elevate your leadership effectiveness.

ASK YOURSELF:

- What trends or developments in my field can I take advantage of to help me grow?
- Are there upcoming projects where I can step up as a leader?
- How can I leverage my strengths in new ways?

EXAMPLES:

- I can adjust my messages to bring different stakeholders on board.
- I can meet experts in AI to keep current.
- I can attend or speak at a conference.

THREATS

External challenges or risks that could hinder your leadership effectiveness.

ASK YOURSELF:

- What is on the horizon that could challenge my ability to lead?
- What forces or factors might hinder my performance or my ability to perform?
- What has threatened me in the past that could resurface as a threat in the future?

EXAMPLES:

- I worry about adapting quickly enough to the changes of technology.
- I am challenged by the disruptions and competition in our industry.
- I am shying away from making decisions.

Personal SWOT

Conduct your personal leadership SWOT on your own and then invite a few trusted friends and colleagues to build on what you have captured.

STRENGTHS Internal factors that I do well as a leader that set me apart from others.	**WEAKNESSES** Internal challenges or areas where I can improve as a leader.
OPPORTUNITIES External factors that can be leveraged to elevate my leadership effectiveness.	**THREATS** External challenges or risks that could hinder my leadership effectiveness.

What Now?

Place a star next to the two areas that need most attention this week. Write down one action for each that you can take in the next 48 hours.

THREE CORE VALUES: Identify three core values that guide your leadership. How do you actively demonstrate these values day-to-day? Where might you fall short of these ideals?

Date:

Defining Your Values

Knowing your personal values is essential for making authentic decisions, guiding priorities, reducing stress, and building a more fulfilling and purpose-driven life. Aligning actions with values not only fosters self-understanding, it enhances resilience and meaningful connections with others.

DIRECTIONS:

Follow these instructions and use the values list on the next page to begin defining your personal values. Please add any value not listed that is relevant and important to you.

1. Eliminate Non-Priority Values
Cross off any values that don't resonate with you or that you're certain don't influence your decisions or hold importance in your life.

2. Identify Priority Values Fundamental to You
Underline the values that resonate with you most. At this point, you may have as many as 15 and that is okay.

3. Write Down Each Value
Write each value on a small index card or you can use post-it-notes. Use one value per card so that you can easily move them around and sort them.

4. Group and Label Similar Values
Group all similar values in a way that makes sense to you. Choose one word within each grouping that best represents the label for the entire group.

5. Select Your Top Six
Select the top six values that reflect the fundamental choices of who you want to be and how you want to show up. Move less important groupings to the side.

6. Explore Your Values In or Out of Action
Capture how you practice, promote, and live each value, and what is challenging about practicing, promoting, and living them.

7. Reinforce and Test Your Values
Look back at the last month or year and reflect on where you have spent your time, energy, and money. Consider how this aligns with the values you've identified.

Defining Your Values

Values List

Abundance	Fairness	Persistence
Accountability	Faith	Personal development
Action	Family	Philanthropy
Adaptability	Flexibility	Physical challenge
Adventure	Freedom	Playfulness
Affection	Friendship	Pleasure
Ambition	Frugality	Power
Art	Fulfillment	Presence
Awareness	Fun	Privacy
Balance	Growth	Public service
Beauty	Happiness	Quality
Bravery	Harmony	Quality relationships
Calmness	Health	Recognition
Change	Helping others	Reputation
Cheerfulness	Honesty	Respect
Clarity	Humility	Security
Comfort	Independence	Self-Respect
Community	Inspiration	Serenity
Compassion	Integrity	Simplicity
Competition	Intelligence	Solitude
Connection	Intimacy	Spirituality
Contribution	Involvement	Spontaneity
Cooperation	Kindness	Stability
Courage	Knowledge	Strength
Creativity	Leadership	Success
Curiosity	Legacy	Teamwork
Decisiveness	Love	Tenacity
Democracy	Loyalty	Tolerance
Determination	Luxury	Truth
Discipline	Meaningful work	Vitality
Efficiency	Merit	Wealth
Empathy	Money	Wellbeing
Energy	Nature	Wisdom
Enthusiasm	Order	Wonder
Ethical practice	Passion	Working with others
Excellence	Peace	Working alone
Excitement	Perfection	Youthfulness

Defining Your Values

Value Labeling and Selection

Defining Your Values

Values in Practice

Value: QUALITY RELATIONSHIPS — Example

How do you practice, promote, and live this value?	What is challenging about practicing, promoting, and living this value?	What agreements will you make with yourself to make sure this value comes to life?
I invest time and energy to develop quality relationships. I proactively support people in my life during highs and lows. I spend money to travel to spend time with people in my life.	Sometimes I focus so much on my relationship with others, I do not set the boundaries I need to give my best self to others. I need to remember that the most important relationship I have is the one with myself.	I will reduce or eliminate the time I spend on relationships that do not bring me joy so that I can pay attention to myself and those who matter most.

Value:

How do you practice, promote, and live this value?	What is challenging about practicing, promoting, and living this value?	What agreements will you make with yourself to make sure this value comes to life?

Value:

How do you practice, promote, and live this value?	What is challenging about practicing, promoting, and living this value?	What agreements will you make with yourself to make sure this value comes to life?

Defining Your Values

Values in Practice Continued

Value:

How do you practice, promote, and live this value?	What is challenging about practicing, promoting, and living this value?	What agreements will you make with yourself to make sure this value comes to life?

Value:

How do you practice, promote, and live this value?	What is challenging about practicing, promoting, and living this value?	What agreements will you make with yourself to make sure this value comes to life?

Value:

How do you practice, promote, and live this value?	What is challenging about practicing, promoting, and living this value?	What agreements will you make with yourself to make sure this value comes to life?

ENERGY TRACKER: Outline the times of day when you feel most energized and when you feel most drained. How can you adjust your schedule to maximize energy and focus?

Date:

User Manual

Think about your personal user manual as a guide to share with others about how you operate and lead, much like a product manual explains its parts and functions. Capture your preferences here.

Conditions I like to work in

Examples

- I work best in quiet spaces
- I like to have the flexibility of working from home

Best way to communicate with me

Example

- Give me the facts without making them sound better than they are.

Things that bother me

Example

- Being late

The way I prefer feedback

Examples

- I like specific examples
- Give suggestions to be better

Preferred hours to work

Example

- After 9 AM M-F

How I think

Example

- I ask questions to see the big picture

What else you need to know

Examples

- I love puzzles, reading, Broadway
- I don't eat mushrooms or meat

Limiting Beliefs

Identify unhelpful thinking patterns that may be reinforcing your limiting beliefs. Gaining clarity is key.

BLACK & WHITE
If I am not perfect, I have failed. Either I do it right or not at all.

MOUNTAIN OUT OF A MOLEHILL
Blowing things out of proportion. Turning disappointment into disaster.

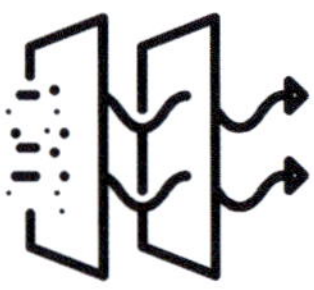

MENTAL FILTER
Zooming in on the bad. Ten good and one bad = dwell on the bad.

EMOTIONAL REASONING
Assuming that because we feel a certain way, it must be true.

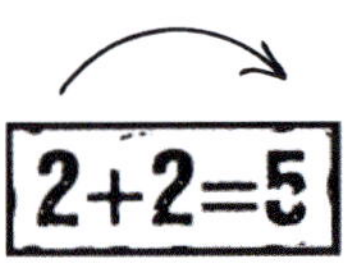

JUMPING TO CONCLUSIONS
Mind reading, imagining we know what others think, or negative forecasting.

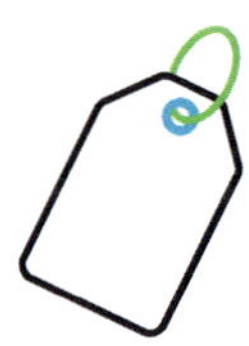

LABELING
Assigning labels to ourselves or other people. "I'm a loser" or "They are completely useless."

OVERGENERALIZING
Seeing a pattern based on a single event. "It is going to be one of THOSE days."

IT'S ALL MY FAULT
Blaming myself for something that was not entirely my fault.

DISQUALIFYING THE POSITIVE
Since there were mistakes, the good does not count.

Which unhelpful ways of thinking can you let go of?

Limiting Beliefs

Limiting beliefs are self-imposed constraints we hold about ourselves and others. Though most are untrue, we unconsciously collect evidence to support them. These beliefs typically form from our interpretation of past experiences and become reinforced through repetitive thinking.

DIRECTIONS

First, identify and highlight any limiting beliefs you're ready to examine more deeply. Then, choose one to create an action plan to overcome this belief on the next page.

LIMITING BELIEFS ABOUT MONEY AND ABUNDANCE

- Making good money requires sacrificing myself
- If I had a better education I could earn more
- I will never get my big break
- There is never enough
- Everyone else gets all the good stuff
- I will never make enough money to support my family
- Money is the root of all evil
- Money doesn't grow on trees
- I just don't know how to manage money
- I am bad with money
- Money is made to be spent
- I will never be rich
- Money turns people rotten
- You can't trust someone with a lot of money
- Money doesn't matter to me
- This always happens to me
- This is all too much for me

LIMITING BELIEFS ABOUT RELATIONSHIPS

- I am useless on my own
- I just have to put up with what I don't like
- Others will hate me if I stand up for myself
- I always get hurt or betrayed
- I am not worthy of being loved
- All the good ones are taken
- My relationships never work out
- I need someone in my life at all times
- I will never find love
- I need someone to take care of me
- I can't do what I want if my family doesn't agree

LIMITING BELIEFS ABOUT WORK

- You can't make money doing what you love
- I am not worthy of that promotion
- I just don't have enough experience
- I am an imposter
- I am not talented
- I have no special strengths
- I am not good enough
- Who would want to hire me?
- Whenever I manage things, it turns out awful
- I never get opportunities to lead big projects
- I will never find the right job
- All bosses are crappy
- My opinion isn't important
- Working for 'the man' is soul crushing
- No one appreciates me
- Asking for help makes me look weak
- Everyone expects too much of me
- I didn't get the promotion again - not fair
- My co-workers don't like me

LIMITING BELIEFS ABOUT SELF-WORTH

- I am a failure
- I can't make things happen
- Things just don't work out for me
- That's just my luck
- I don't deserve everything I want

LIMITING BELIEFS ABOUT GOOD HEALTH

- I don't have time with all the work I have to do
- My body just heals slowly
- Getting sick is unavoidable
- I'm destined to struggle with my weight forever
- I can't help myself, I like the good stuff

Limiting Beliefs

Use the chart to work through your most restrictive limiting belief.

Example

YOUR IDEAL STATEMENT

My vision is to live in London one day and apply my marketing expertise in an international setting, contributing to innovative campaigns and global brand strategies.

Barriers to My Ideal Write down every barrier that is keeping you from your idea.	Opposites of My Barriers Turn the barriers into the opposite statement with a positive message.	Applying Future Shifts If the second column is now true, what you will do differently?
Examples • I don't have a visa. • This is too risky. • My experience is limited. • Who would hire me? • London has enough people like me.	Examples • Taking a risk means I am growing and learning. • I have a solid 5 years of experience I can offer. • My manager says I was his best hire of the year. • London needs me.	Examples • I will proactively connect with people who live and work in London. • I will ask to be involved in the next global project. • I will research what is needed to make a move.

YOUR IDEAL STATEMENT

Barriers to My Ideal Write down every barrier that is keeping you from your idea.	Opposites of My Barriers Turn the barriers into the opposite statement with a positive message.	Applying Future Shifts If the second column is now true, what you will do differently?

BLIND SPOT: Write a letter to your future self describing how you transformed a current leadership blind spot into a strength. What specific feedback sparked this growth, and what steps did you take to get there?

Date:

Know - Do - Be

Reflect on these three questions to enhance your self-awareness, personal growth, and leadership development.

KNOW

What do you KNOW about?

Consider the areas where you have knowledge, expertise, or insight.

NOW WHAT?

Where can you shift what you know into action in your personal or professional life?

DO

What do you DO with what you already know?

Think about how you apply the knowledge you have collected over time.

NOW WHAT?

How can you build on what you are doing so that it becomes second nature?

BE

What has become a part of your BEING?

Reflect on actions or habits you practice so consistently that they are part of you.

NOW WHAT?

How might you shift away from something that no longer serves you or others?

EMOTION MAP: What emotions have you experienced today? List them out and add what led to each emotion and how it shaped your interactions with others.

Date:

Avoidance Behaviors Defined

These behaviors can show up as potential avoidance statements because they can be used to sidestep or postpone dealing with difficult issues, emotions, or conversations. Not all the statements are inherently problematic and can be genuinely used in appropriate contexts. They become an issue when they are used repeatedly or inappropriately to evade addressing important topics or emotions.

Deflecting
Redirects attention away from the main issue or shifts the subject or focus to unrelated points.

Delegating
Passes off responsibility to avoid direct engagement or having to take responsibility.

Delaying
Pushes the issue to a later time in the week, month, or an ambiguous time in the future.

Dismissing
Ignores the problem in the hopes that it will resolve itself in its own time.

Displacing
Prioritizes other matters over this one to avoid addressing the current issue.

Downplaying
Treats a topic or challenge as minor to avoid dealing with it in the moment.

Excusing
Offers explanations to reduce the perceived responsibility to avoid blame or accountability.

Justifying
Portrays a situation or behavior as acceptable or understandable, even if it is not ideal.

Minimizing
Makes it seem like immediate attention is not required, important, or would have an impact.

Overcomplicating
Overcomplicates an issue or uses hypotheticals to stall.

Overlooking
Fails to notice or consider something important or bypasses critical details.

Postponing
Defers taking action to prevent progress or allows an issue to linger.

Presenting as 'Fine'
Uses surface-level composure to avoid discussing deeper issues.

Refocusing
Redirects to avoid the topic, challenge or issue at hand.

Requesting
Claims that more information is required to evaluate even though all data is presented.

Rationalizing
Creates seemingly reasonable explanations to avoid guilt, doubt, or accountability.

Self-Justifying
Using personal reasoning to justify why you are or are not doing something.

Shifting Responsibility
Claims it is not in their domain or area.

Avoidance Behavior Bingo

Bring this bingo board to a meeting and track how often you observe one of these behaviors or hear one of the phrases. Capture how you or others react when hearing them.

BINGO

Minimalizing	"Let's circle back to this another day."	Justifying	"There are too many factors to consider."	Dismissing
"I can handle it."	Displacing	"That is not my area."	Deflecting	"It's never been a problem before."
Judging	"I am fine on the outside."	Downplaying	"This is just how it is done here."	Excusing
"Let's discuss this at our next meeting."	Over-complicating	"This usually works itself out."	Self-Justification	"Let's take this offline."
Rationalizing	"We need more context to decide."	Redirecting	"Why don't we look at what is going well."	Delegating

Avoiding Avoidance Behavior

Let's look in the mirror now. To avoid using the avoidance behaviors that may show up from time to time, check which actions would benefit you.

- [ ] Acknowledge and validate concerns raised by team members to show you take their input seriously.
- [ ] Admit mistakes or shortcomings when appropriate and focus on solutions over justifications.
- [ ] Address issues promptly and honestly, using clear and specific language to ensure understanding.
- [ ] Be open to discussing tough or uncomfortable topics.
- [ ] Explicitly recognize the importance of problems.
- [ ] Ask clarifying and probing questions to ensure you grasp the full context and uncover underlying concerns.
- [ ] Establish next steps with clear timelines, assigned responsibilities, and regular check-ins for accountability.
- [ ] Listen fully to others' perspectives and respond empathetically to their emotions.
- [ ] Gently address avoidance statements when they arise, whether from yourself or others.
- [ ] Pay attention to patterns in the way you respond, especially in challenging situations.

JOY LIST: List what brings you joy and makes you feel truly alive.

Date:

Story of Your Name

Telling the story of your name is a way to connect with others by sharing a piece of your background, values, and personal identity, offering insight into how you see yourself or how you wish to be seen.

When you share the story of your name, consider:

- Cultural or familial significance
- Origins, meaning, or family connections
- How it has shaped your identity
- Nicknames
- Unique experiences
- Meaningful or funny stories
- Changes or shifts to your name over time

My name is Judith Ann Goldberg, though most know me as Judy, or for certain people sometimes Juch, Judes, Goldie, Noodles or Goldberger. My name has German and Jewish roots, with Judith meaning "praised one" and Goldberg symbolizing a "gold mountain."

Judith Ann Goldberg

Judith Ann was reserved for my parents and typically meant I had been naughty. And while I haven't heard anyone say "Judy, Judy, Judy" quite like Cary Grant, the nickname has a place in pop culture that makes my name repeated like this when people meet me.

Recognizing Stress Cues

Leaders must recognize that everyone experiences stress differently. Awareness of these differences allows you to offer the specific support and communication tactics each person needs to cope and move forward.

Thinking Preferences	What you might observe about others under stress	What others might need from you to progress
Analytical	• Appears overly skeptical or judgmental • Questions expertise • Responds curtly	• Ensure accuracy • Let them share thoughts and questions • Share facts and rationale
Structural	• Develops own plan to take control • Appears to be rigid • Nit-picks content	• Appreciate their attention to the details • Clarify what needs immediate attention • Minimize surprises
Social	• Acts overly emotional • Fixates on the impact to others • Takes things personally	• Ask how they are feeling • Show sincerity • Explore how to address concerns in line with goals
Conceptual	• Seems disconnected • Proposes farfetched ideas • Imagines negative potential possibilities	• Involve them in brainstorming • Skip the details • Anchor them in specific tasks in the moment
Ranges of Behaviors	• From looking bored or aloof to overly dismissive • From appearing passive to prioritizing own agenda • From reaffirming and intensifying efforts to acting uncertain or avoiding	• Share information ahead and/or provide options for feedback and discussion • Create a safe space and/or embrace healthy conflict • Provide clarity on finalized decisions vs. those still open for input

Source: Emergenetics® International

Chapter Reflection: Scan Yourself

Today's Date:

An insight or thought I've had this chapter is...

____

____

____

____

____

____

Where in your body did you feel this chapter the most?

A pattern I've noticed about myself is...

I want to talk with someone more about...

____

____

____

Capture an image or picture that best represents this chapter.

A song title for this chapter would be...

Harness Your Integrity

Words of Wonder

"The time is always right to do what is right."
– Martin Luther King Jr.

"You may not control all the events that happen to you, but you can decide not to be reduced by them."
– Maya Angelou

"You teach people how to treat you by what you allow, what you stop, and what you reinforce."
– Tony Gaskins

Harness Your Integrity

What does this chapter cover?

Clarify your decision-making frameworks, determine which boundaries to establish or release, identify feedback to act upon, and practice intentionality in your words and actions.

Why does this matter?

Studies by Daniel Goleman, author of "Emotional Intelligence," point to the positive effects of leaders who practice self-awareness and intentionality in their words and actions. Staying true to your values and principles is crucial for long-term organizational success and creates a more productive and engaged workforce.

What will you gain?

The ability to stand firm in your integrity. This clarity reduces decision fatigue, fosters a deeper connection to what truly matters, and leads to more efficient and harmonious work.

EXERCISES

- In 10 Words
- Leadership Philosophy
- Balancing Commitments
- Launch and Adjust
- Ethics of Leadership
- Introducing Yourself
- Presenting Yourself
- Boundary Setting
- Recentering
- Whispering Rules

WRITING PROMPTS

- Guiding Others
- Internal Compass
- Observe Yourself
- Letter to Your Team
- Lessons Applied

GUIDING OTHERS: When has someone turned to you for guidance? How did you guide them?

Date:

In 10 Words

Use 10 nouns and/or adjectives to complete the sentence for each row and column in the grid.

	I am...	I am not...
If you asked me...		
If you asked my peers or co-workers...		
If you asked my friends...		
If you asked my family...		
If you asked my children or young people in my life...		

What Now?

Select 2-3 attributes or characteristics you'd like to amplify and share more with your colleagues and teams. What will this look like in action?

Leadership Philosophy

Your leadership philosophy defines who you are as a leader. It highlights your unique characteristics, values, and guiding principles. Capture answers to the questions using simple, direct language, then write out your leadership philosophy on a separate page.

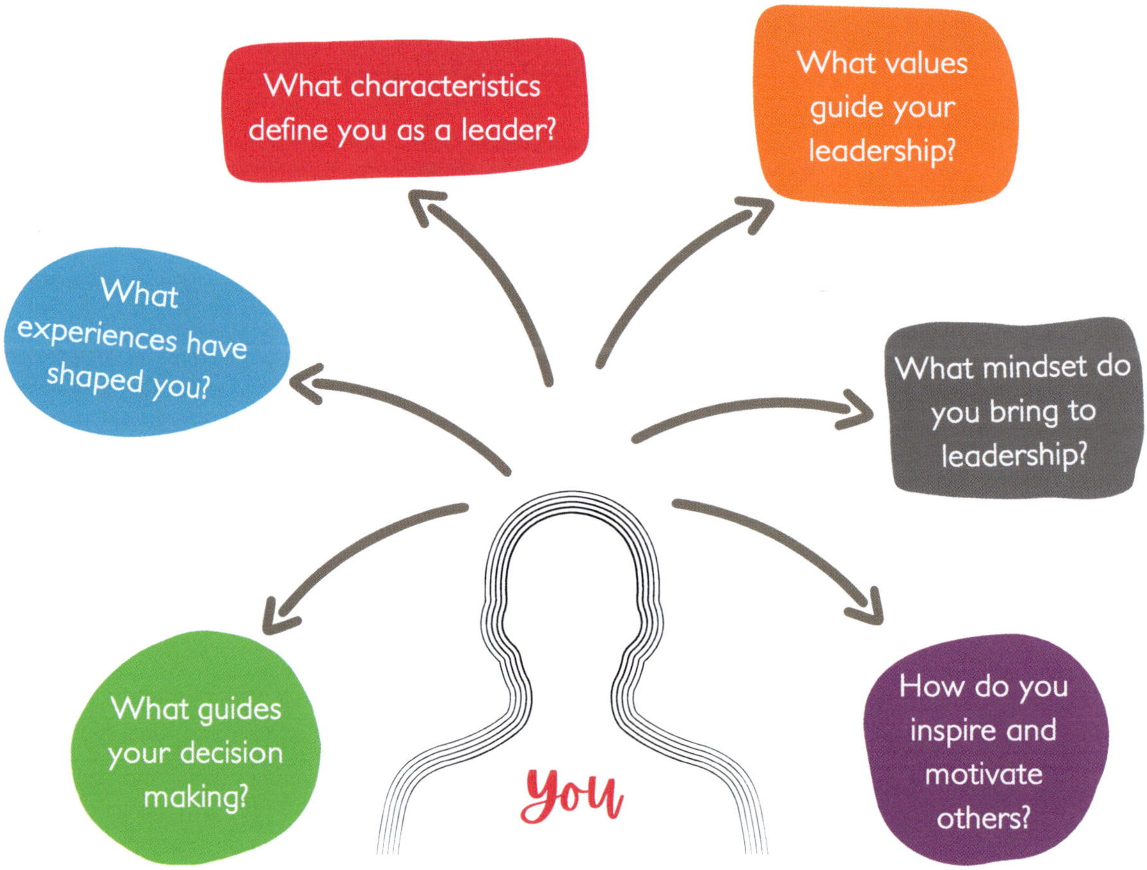

What Now?

Once you have your leadership philosophy written out, consider the actions you have taken in the past year. Do the actions align with your leadership philosophy? If not, what can you do to ensure that your actions are more aligned with your philosophy moving forward?

Leadership Philosophy

Each of these leaders has crafted and embodied a philosophy that reflects their unique approach to leadership. Their philosophies have been studied, shared, and adopted by leaders worldwide for their clarity and impact.

Colin Powell

The former U.S. Secretary of State and military leader, Colin Powell's leadership philosophy centered on resilience, adaptability, and maintaining perspective under pressure. His "13 Rules of Leadership" emphasized the importance of clear decision-making and ethical conduct.

Indra Nooyi

As the former CEO of PepsiCo, Indra Nooyi's leadership philosophy revolves around "Performance with Purpose." She emphasized long-term strategy, employee empowerment, and humility, while advocating for lifelong learning, mentorship, and work-life balance.

Simone Biles

Simone Biles' leadership philosophy emphasizes self-care, vulnerability, and prioritizing mental health. She has demonstrated that effective leadership involves acknowledging limits and encouraging a supportive, open community.

Nelson Mandela

Nelson Mandela's leadership philosophy was grounded in forgiveness, reconciliation, and leading by example. His approach emphasized empathy, moral authority, and the commitment to justice, making him a global symbol of servant leadership.

Jack Welch

The former CEO of General Electric, Jack Welch's leadership philosophy was performance-driven and focused on candor, simplicity, and differentiation. He believed in delivering results, simplifying processes, and fostering transparent communication.

Ruth Bader Ginsburg

As a former U.S. Supreme Court Justice, Ruth Bader Ginsburg's leadership philosophy was anchored in perseverance, equality, and justice. She believed in leading with integrity and advocated for dissenting opinions as a form of leadership and a voice for the underrepresented.

Sheryl Sandberg

Sheryl Sandberg's leadership philosophy, as outlined in her book Lean In, is rooted in empowerment and gender equality. She advocates for women to take initiative, advocate for themselves, and pursue leadership roles in the workplace.

Simon Sinek

Simon Sinek's leadership philosophy, embodied in his concept of "Start with Why," focuses on creating a motivating vision and clearly communicating the purpose behind actions to inspire followers and drive collective action.

Colin Powell's Philosophy

Colin Powell's 13 Rules of Leadership are packed with powerful insights. They offer wise reminders to stay grounded, manage emotions, and lead by example to guide your team through challenges with resilience and integrity.

1 **It ain't as bad as you think!**
It will look better in the morning. Leaving the office at night with a winning attitude affects more than you alone; it conveys that attitude to your followers.

2 **Get mad, then get over it.**
Instead of letting anger destroy you, use it to make constructive change.

3 **Avoid having your ego so close to your position that when your position falls, your ego goes with it.**
Keep your ego in check, and know that you can lead from wherever you are.

4 **It can be done.**
Leaders make things happen. If one approach doesn't work, find another.

5 **Be careful what you choose. You may get it.**
Your team will have to live with your choices, so don't rush.

6 **Don't let adverse facts stand in the way of a good decision.**
Superb leadership is often a matter of superb instinct. When faced with a tough decision, use the time available to gather information that will inform your instinct.

7 **You can't make someone else's choices. You shouldn't let someone else make yours.**
While good leaders listen and consider all perspectives, they ultimately make their own decisions. Accept your good decisions. Learn from your mistakes.

8 **Check small things.**
Followers live in the world of small things. Find ways to get visibility into that world.

9 **Share credit.**
People need recognition and a sense of worth as much as they need food and water.

10 **Remain calm. Be kind.**
Few people make sound or sustainable decisions in an atmosphere of chaos. Establish a calm zone while maintaining a sense of urgency.

11 **Have a vision. Be demanding.**
Followers need to know where their leaders are taking them and for what purpose. To achieve the purpose, set demanding standards and make sure they are met.

12 **Don't take counsel of your fears or naysayers.**
Successful organizations are not built by cowards or cynics.

13 **Perpetual optimism is a force multiplier.**
If you believe and have prepared your followers, your followers will believe.

Balancing Commitments

Balancing commitments means making intentional choices to prioritize and manage responsibilities, focusing time and energy on what matters most. It involves aligning actions with priorities, while maintaining well-being and nurturing key relationships.

Review how you are tracking your tasks. Is anything falling through the cracks? What adjustments are needed?

Examine the way you organize your week. What patterns do you notice? What might need to shift?

Explore where you can combine tasks to streamline priorities. What would your team recommend?

Evaluate new opportunities or requests before taking them on. What should you be saying no to right now?

Assess your progress on achieving your revenue goals. Where might you need to adjust to stay on track?

Experiment with productivity features like focus modes. What are you willing to test out for a couple of weeks?

INTERNAL COMPASS: In the face of a difficult decision, what internal compass guides your choices? Write about a recent challenge and how you stayed true to your principles.

Date:

Launch and Adjust

As a leader, the "right" decision may not always be immediately clear or available. Instead of letting this lead to inaction, trust that you can still decide to act and make any decision work through how you respond. Use the "Launch and Adjust" map below to guide you.

1

LAUNCH
Begin a new initiative or project.

2

FEEDBACK
Capture data, observations, team input.

3

ADJUST
Refine, make changes, iterate.

4

RE - LAUNCH
Start a new cycle.

GO BACK TO
THE BEGINNING

Ethics of Leadership

The ethics of leadership refers to the moral principles, values, and behaviors that guide leaders in their decisions and actions. Ethical leadership is about doing what is right, fair, and just, even when it is challenging or unpopular.

DIRECTIONS:
Read and respond to each scenario presented.

SCENARIO ONE

Your top-performing employee has violated a minor company policy. Reporting the violation could impact morale and performance, but not reporting it undermines the company's principles.

What would you do and how would you defend your decision?

SCENARIO TWO

Your organization must make difficult layoffs to meet budget constraints and you are faced with a critical decision. You can let go of five newer, promising employees or two long-standing employees who are well respected but not as effective in their roles.

What would you do and how would you defend your decision?

Ethics of Leadership

SCENARIO THREE

You signed off without carefully reviewing a new contract that had a major mistake, potentially costing your organization a $1,000 fine or damaging its reputation. Once you realize the error, you can inform your stakeholders about the mistake or you can attempt to rectify the issue quietly, possibly delaying disclosure and hoping no one notices.

What would you do and how would you defend your decision?

CHALLENGE

Remember your core values when faced with these ethical challenges. They will guide you to make the best decision with the information you have in the moment.

- Competing Priorities: When you have to balance profitability, stakeholder demands, and ethical principles.
- Gray Areas: When you have to navigate complex situations without clear "right" or "wrong" answers.
- Pressure to Perform: When you are facing pressure to compromise ethics to meet short-term goals.
- Diverse Perspectives: When you are managing differing views of, "What is 'ethical?'" in multicultural or global teams.

What now?

How well do your answers to these scenarios align with the values you identified on pages 12 and 13?

Introducing Yourself

The way you introduce yourself creates a strong first impression, ensures people catch your name correctly, and makes it easier for them to remember you.

What feels like the most authentic and clear way to introduce yourself? Would it be helpful to use pronunciation guidance on your emails or virtual platforms? Is there anything that could help others get to know you better?

HELLO
MY NAME IS

Hello, I'm Thabo Ndlovu, Taa-boh Nd-loh-voo. Please call me Thabo. So nice to meet you!

List a few useful professional facts about yourself.

List a few personal facts about yourself you are willing to share.

List the ways you might respond to the question, "What do you do?"

Presenting Yourself

How you present yourself when meeting others is important, as it sets the tone for connection. Use this page to gain clarity and confidently prepare for any interaction.

What sets you apart from others?

What inspires you about your own work?

What is a goal you are willing to share?

List out a few back-pocket questions you can ask others.

What Now?

Practice introducing and presenting yourself with friends and colleagues until you feel comfortable and authentic in the way you are showing up and sharing with others.

OBSERVE YOURSELF: Record yourself speaking about a project you're passionate about. As you review the video, jot down words, phrases, or body language that stand out as authentic or inspiring.

Date:

Boundary Setting

Maintaining parameters in our own lives takes reflection, commitment, confidence and practice. Boundaries empower us to build more harmonious relationships and move through our lives with greater ease.

These visible and easy-to-spot boundaries are well-understood and fairly obvious. Most of us accept, respect, and abide by them.

DIRECTIONS:

Because not all boundaries are visible and easy to spot, consider the boundaries you hope to have in place for all areas of your life but somehow are often crossed. This could be at work, at home, in relationships, or in the community.

MY SIGNALS What signal tells you a boundary of yours has been crossed?	MY ACTION What will you say next time it happens? What else can you do?
E.g., Consider when you experience resentment, irritability, anger, and/or emotional discomfort. Or feel a tightening in your body, a rapid heart rate, or simply know that something is off, even if you can't pinpoint it.	E.g., Pinpoint the trigger. Was it the action, person, or request? Could you say, "No thanks," "I need a few minutes to gather my thoughts," or "I would appreciate you not bringing that up again."

Boundary Setting

Becoming aware of the boundaries spectrum can help you understand where boundaries may need to be set or released.

DIRECTIONS:
Review the boundaries spectrum and then check any statement you might identify with under each type of boundary.

What are Healthy Boundaries?
When you confidently and truthfully say "yes" or "no" and feel good about it, and when you are okay when others say "no" to you.

HEALTHY

POROUS

RIGID

What are Unhealthy Boundaries?
When you say "yes" when you really mean "no" and end up feeling anger, resentment, drained, overwhelmed, or frequently complain.

POROUS

I tend to...

- ☐ Overshare personal information
- ☐ Have difficulty saying "no" to others' requests
- ☐ Get over involved with others' problems
- ☐ Become dependent on the opinions and input of others
- ☐ Tolerate abuse or disrespect

HEALTHY

I tend to...

- ☐ Accept when others say "no"
- ☐ Stand firm in my values and beliefs
- ☐ Share personal info appropriately
- ☐ Clearly communicate and know my personal wants and needs
- ☐ Make time for self-care without apologizing

RIGID

I tend to...

- ☐ Avoid intimacy and close relationships
- ☐ Avoid asking for help
- ☐ Be very protective of personal information
- ☐ Detach myself, even with romantic partners
- ☐ React in a defensive manner

What is coming up for you as you observe your checkmarks?

Boundary Setting

Consider your boundaries for each category (personal life, professional life, and relationships). Write in specific examples of porous, healthy or rigid boundaries for each area and the impact this boundary has on your life or leadership.

Boundary Type	Personal	Professional	Relationships
 **POROUS** too weak, allowing others to take advantage			
 **HEALTHY** balanced, respecting both your needs and others'			
 **RIGID** too strict, potentially preventing connection			

What Now?

Assess your chart to determine which boundary work is most needed right now. Commit to taking one action toward moving in the direction you desire.

LETTER TO YOUR TEAM: Write a letter to your team explaining one thing you did today to honor your boundaries and why it matters to you as a leader.

Date:

Recentering

Somatic exercises are proven to release tension and strengthen your mind-body connection. This exercise only takes a moment and invites you to bring awareness to your senses, helping you to recenter quickly to regain control, find calm, and refocus.

START BY TAKING 10 DEEP BREATHES

Name 5 things you can SEE in this moment.

Name 4 things you can HEAR in this moment.

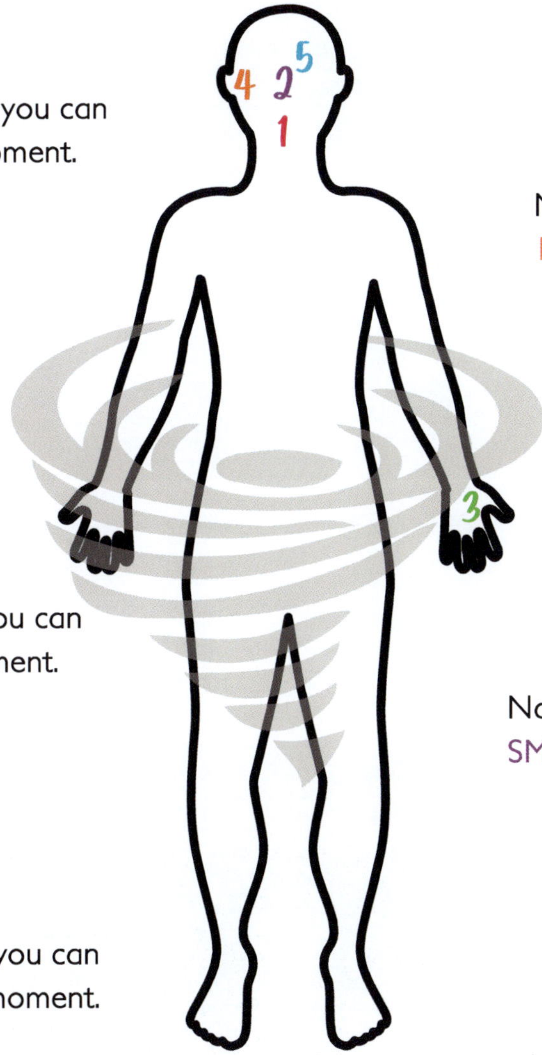

Name 3 things you can FEEL in this moment.

Name 2 things you can SMELL in this moment.

Name 1 thing you can TASTE in this moment.

What Now?

Choose one of the things you named, and use all of the other senses available to you to describe it. What does it smell like? Taste like? Look like? Sound like? Feel like? Come back to this exercise in moments of unease or flurry.

LESSONS APPLIED: Write a letter to a mentor who exemplified integrity through their actions. Include the lessons they taught you and explain how you apply those lessons in your own leadership.

Date:

Whispering Rules

As you move through the week, listen for all of the self-imposed rules you are whispering to yourself. Keep a running list and capture each one.

Examples

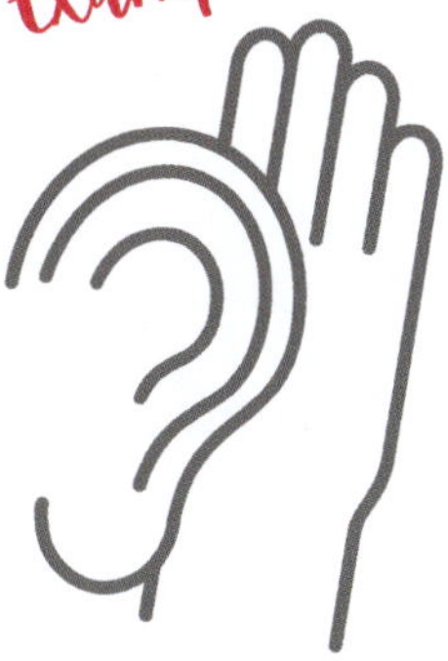

"I must always have the answers."

"It's my job to make tough decisions."

"Don't take things personally."

"As the leader, I must always be in control."

"Don't let them see your emotions."

What Now?

Examine the whispering rules you have listed. Are they helpful or holding you back? Commit to revisiting, breaking, or letting go of them.

Chapter Reflection: Harness Your Integrity

Today's Date:

An insight or thought I've had this chapter is...

Where in your body did you feel this chapter the most?

A pattern I've noticed about myself is...

Capture an image or picture that best represents this chapter.

I want to talk with someone more about...

A song title for this chapter would be...

Invest your Time

Words of Wonder

"The way we spend our time defines who we are."
– Jonathan Estrin

"Investing in yourself is the best investment you will ever make. It will not only improve your life, it will improve the lives of all those around you."
– Robin Sharma

"It's not about having time.
It's about making time."
– Unknown

Invest Your Time

What does this chapter cover?

Concentrate on where your energy, time and money is allocated, learn to set priorities for yourself and your team, adapt where you need to, and prioritize self-care to align with your values and guiding principles.

Why does this matter?

A leader's ability to prioritize time, energy, and resources effectively will directly influence team success, decision-making, and alignment with organizational goals.

What will you gain?

Over time, you will create a thriving, value-driven culture that contributes to both personal and organizational growth and leads to long-term success and resilience.

EXERCISES

- Elevate Your Brain Power
- Comfort-Stretch-Panic Zone
- Write A Leader Review
- Release Your Armor
- Amplify Your Leadership
- Mentoring
- Your Behaviors Matter
- Wellbeing Assessment
- Making the Most of Your 1:1s
- Amplifying 1:1s
- Question Shifting
- Take A Field Trip

WRITING PROMPTS

- Two Sides of Health
- New Skill Insight
- Feedback Spark
- Letter of Gratitude
- Now is the Time

Elevate Your Brain Power

The prefrontal cortex makes thousands of decisions a day. Where you focus your attention, how you respond to challenges, and how you prioritize information all shape your capacity as a leader.

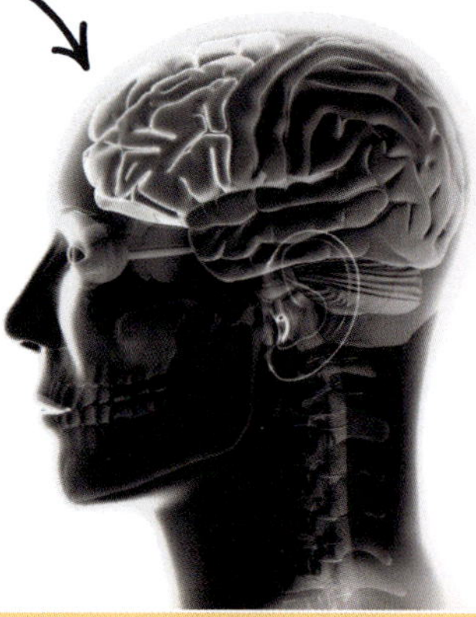

The prefrontal cortex (PFC) is a critical area of the brain located at the front of the frontal lobe. It governs high-level cognitive skills and takes in over 11 million bits of information every second, filtering and processing them to guide decision-making, problem-solving, emotional regulation, social behavior, and impulse control.

Here's what every leader should know about the PFC, why it matters, and what you can do to maximize it.

WHAT TO KNOW	WHAT TO DO
Decision-Making & Problem-Solving: Helps us analyze information and make smart decisions.	Make sure to take breaks during complex decision-making to refresh mental clarity.
Emotional Control: Manages emotional responses, helping us stay calm under pressure.	Practice mindfulness or breathing exercises to handle stress and respond thoughtfully.
Impulse Control: Allows us to pause and consider before reacting.	Pause briefly before responding to challenging situations to think through your actions.
Empathy & Social Skills: Helps us read social cues and connect with others.	Take time to listen actively and understand your team's perspectives to build trust.
Creativity & Innovation: Supports creative thinking.	Set aside time for brainstorming and creative thinking to inspire new ideas.
Managing Mental Fatigue: Tires quickly if overused, leading to decision fatigue.	Schedule regular breaks and rest periods to maintain mental energy and sharpness.

Contributor: Phil Dobson, Author of "The Brain Book: How to Think & Work Smarter" and Founder of BrainWorkshops

TWO SIDES OF HEALTH: On the left side of the page, list everything you currently do to support your physical, mental, and emotional health. On the right side, list what you could add or do more of. Which will you commit to first?

Date:

Comfort-Stretch-Panic Zone

The Comfort-Stretch-Panic Model was popularized by George Leonard, one of the founders of the Human Potential Movement. In his book he discusses how individuals progress through stages of comfort, stretch, and panic in the process of learning and personal development.

Comfort Zone

This zone is where people feel most safe, familiar, and at ease. They are operating within their existing capabilities and routines, which may lead to feeling confident or protected. Some may be bored or under-stimulated.

Ready to leave your comfort zone?

Identify one thing you can take on that feels slightly challenging but manageable.

Set a goal that moves you toward a new experience or skill.

Seek feedback from others to uncover areas where you might grow.

Stretch Zone

This zone represents a stage of moderate discomfort or challenge, where people are working in a more active, demanding or uncertain environment. It may lead to feelings of nervousness or excitement as people confront new tasks or experiences.

Ready to embrace the stretch zone?

Stay focused on the opportunity rather than the discomfort.

Build confidence by celebrating small wins along the way.

Seek support from mentors, colleagues, or resources to navigate challenges.

Panic Zone

This zone reflects a state of heightened anxiety or overwhelm, where people may feel out of their depth, scared or stressed by the demands placed upon them. Some may not be able to learn effectively in this environment or will have the urge to retreat.

Ready to explore the panic zone?

Pause, assess, and ask yourself what is causing the panic.

Focus on what's immediately doable or seek help to reduce the pressure.

Practice deep breathing or mindfulness to regain clarity.

What now?

Use this model to assess your team's growth. Identify where they are and adjust challenges and development opportunities to keep them engaged and productive.

NEW SKILL INSIGHT: What new skill or insight have you recently gained, and how has applying it impacted you?

Date:

Write A Leader Review

Listen to a TedTalk, Podcast or other media on a topic of your choice related to leadership. Write a review using the prompts.

What was the highlight?

What are three things you learned?

What will you do as a result of listening or watching?

What would you like to have been different?

What now?

Write your review on the next page. Share it with a colleague and offer them the same review prompts so they can write a review for you. Compare your reviews.

Write A Leader Review

Use your notes to write a review that can be shared with others.

Example

Nov 2022

Great leadership is a network, not a hierarchy

Gitte Frederiksen

Review of "Great Leadership is a Network, Not a Hierarchy" by Gitte Frederiksen

The highlight for me was Frederiksen's fresh approach to leadership as a network. This concept breaks the typical hierarchical mold and focuses on creating connected, supportive teams where everyone feels empowered. The emphasis on relationships and collaboration really stood out.

After watching, I plan to focus on building stronger, more open connections within my team. I'll prioritize fostering a collaborative environment over reinforcing traditional roles. It would have been helpful to see more examples of companies implementing this approach, giving practical insights into how networked leadership works in different settings.

My takeaways are:

- Leadership as a network encourages shared responsibility and enhances innovation.
- Team members feel more valued when they are part of decision-making.

Overall, this talk is thought-provoking and a must-watch for anyone rethinking team dynamics and leadership structure.

FEEDBACK SPARK: Think of a time when someone's feedback sparked a change in you. What was it, and how did you respond?

Date:

Release Your Armor

Scan the QR Code and listen to Part One of Dr. Brené Brown's two-part podcast on Armored versus Daring Leadership.

Dear Me,

After listening to the first part of Dr. Brown's podcast on Armored versus Daring Leadership, I am ready to take some action. So here I am, ready to commit, to let go, and get vulnerable so that I can become a braver, more daring leader.

The Armored Leadership I'm going to let go of is…

Letting go!

I've recognized that holding onto this armor impacts…

If I let go of ______________________________
I will be able to…

The first action I will take is…

You got this!

Me

Amplify Your Leadership

Scan the QR Code and listen to Part Two of Dr. Brené Brown's two-part podcast on Armored versus Daring Leadership.

Dear Me,

After listening to the second part of Dr. Brown's podcast, I am ready to amplify and develop the skills I need to become a braver, more daring leader.

To become a more daring leader, I will develop ways to amplify how I …

- ☐ Rumble with vulnerability so I can show up without my armor.
- ☐ Live into my values.
- ☐ Bravely trust and assume the best about people's intent, motivation and behavior.
- ☐ Learn to rise to overcome mistakes, face hurt, and learn from failure.

Time to Amplify!

By amplifying/developing this skill I believe I will…

My team will benefit because…

The first action I will take is…

I will ask ______________________________ to hold me accountable, call me out, and celebrate with me as I become a braver, more daring leader.

Let's do this!

Me

LETTER OF GRATITUDE: Write a letter to someone who has significantly invested in your growth and success. Share how their guidance, support, or belief in you has shaped your journey.

Date:

Mentoring

Mentoring helps individuals navigate complexities, build resilience, and adapt to change—skills that are indispensable for effective leadership.

5x Mentees are promoted five times more often than those who do not have mentors, and mentors are six times more likely to get promoted.
Source: A 2007 study conducted by Gartner and Capital Analytics at Sun Microsystems.

87% of mentors and mentees feel empowered by their mentoring relationships and have developed greater confidence. **87%**
Source: A 2024 Study by Moving Ahead and Deloitte

When you think of the word "mentor," what two qualities or characteristics come to mind?

Which statement resonates most with you about mentorship?

- ○ A mentor is a guide who shares wisdom.
- ○ A mentor is a partner in problem-solving.
- ○ A mentor is a source of inspiration and encouragement.
- ○ A mentor challenges someone to grow.

Rank your confidence in these mentoring skills
(1 = most confident, 5 = least confident):

____ Building trust and rapport
____ Providing constructive feedback
____ Guiding someone through challenges
____ Listening actively and empathetically
____ Helping others clarify their goals

What personal strength will you lean on most as a mentor, and why?

Mentoring

Circle the insights you could provide as a mentor.

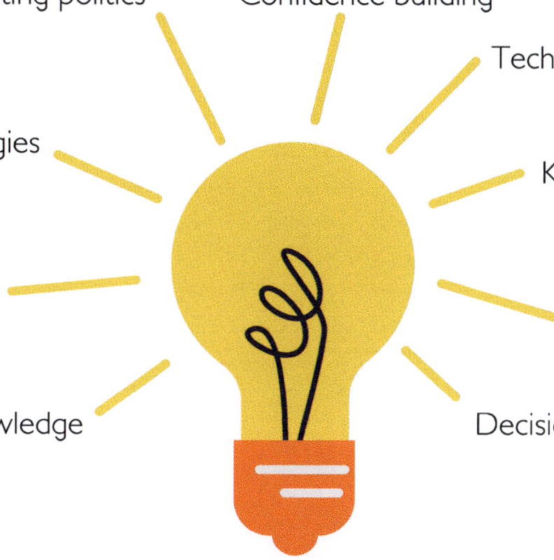

Mark on the scale how ready you are to dedicate time to a mentoring relationship.

1 2 3 4 5 6 7 8 9 10

Not now · Getting there · Within reach · Ready now

If time is a barrier, what adjustments could you make to prioritize mentoring?

Imagine it's five years from now, and a former mentee thanks you. What do you want them to say you helped them accomplish?

What Now?

Identify potential mentees you'd like to work with and why. Decide what kind of support you can offer and set a meeting to create a mentorship action plan.

NOW IS THE TIME: Write a letter to yourself about the conversations you've been holding off on. What's keeping you from taking action?

Date:

Your Behaviors Matter

Identify 2–4 key behaviors you exhibit as a leader (e.g., communication style, decision-making approach, how you provide feedback, etc.). Be specific about each behavior and how it might impact your team's performance and well-being.

In a Wondershift study, 440 participants shared their experiences with leaders exhibiting undesirable behaviors. Nearly 60% reported feeling consistently on edge, while 12% experienced physical and mental health symptoms, including depression, anxiety, and nausea.

Your Behavior	Impact to Your Team (+ / -)
Example I prefer quick decisions rather than prolonged discussions.	Quick decisions may lead to faster progress. (+) Without adequate discussion, some team members might not feel they can express their views or fully commit to the outcome. (-)

What Now?

Send an anonymous survey to your team to gain their feedback on these behaviors to check if your self assessment matches their perspectives.

Wellbeing Assessment

Your mental fitness and wellbeing as a leader is critical. Evaluate your current state in different wellbeing areas and identify where you are thriving and where your attention is needed. Check the box that best describes your current state today.

Today's date is ______________

Current State	1 Struggling	2 Adjusting	3 Growing	4 Thriving
Sleep & Rest				
Physical Activity				
Stress Management				
Emotional Awareness				
Relationships & Social Support				
Purpose & Fulfillment				
Nutrition & Hydration				
Fun & Creativity				

What will you improve this month? Pick 1-2 areas. For each, choose one doable action step.

Example

Stress Management		
Practice 5 minutes of mindfulness daily.		

What Now?

Mark your calendar to take this assessment again in three months' time.

Making the Most of Your 1:1s

Each meeting has a distinct purpose - whether it's to develop an employee, solve a problem, check in on a project, strengthen a relationship, or collect feedback. Use this chart to distinguish the type of discussion you will have.

Type	Purpose	Sample Questions
1:1 Onboarding	To set up a new employee for success, build a relationship, and introduce the company's values, goals, and expectations.	• What does success look like for you in 30 days? • How can I best partner with you to achieve this? • What are your thoughts on our mission and values? • What is the best way for us to communicate? • What questions do you have?
1:1 Stay Interviews*	To understand what keeps an employee engaged and committed to the team and company.	• What do you like most about working here? • What are you learning and enjoying? • What would you change about your job if you could? • What talents are you not fully utilizing in your role? • What can I do to support your career goals?
1:1 Weekly or Monthly	To provide feedback and support, discuss progress on goals and projects, address any concerns, and set priorities for the coming week or month.	• On a scale of 1-10, how would you rate your personal wellbeing? • What is the highlight/lowlight of this week/month? • What feels harder than it should right now? • Are there any blockers I can help remove? • What could I experiment with doing differently this month to help you more?
1:1 Quarterly Goal Setting	To set specific and measurable goals, and develop a plan to achieve them.	• In what ways would you like to grow as a professional? • What additional clarity do you need on your goals? • What questions do you have about your KPIs? • What's one thing I can start, stop, and continue doing to help you achieve your goals?
1:1 Performance Meeting	To review performance and expectations, provide feedback, and learn what works and what could be better.	• Where did we/you succeed? Fall short? Learn? • What do you want to accomplish in the next quarter? • What might prevent you from hitting your goals? • What questions, if answered, would help you day-to-day?
1:1 Coaching	To provide ongoing support and guidance.	• What motivates and inspires you to do your best work? • On a scale of 1-10, how would you rate your time here? • How can we work together more effectively as a team?
1:1 Emergency	To address an urgent situation or issue that requires immediate attention.	• What immediate support, guidance, or resources do you need? • How have you navigated situations like this before? • How can we work together to address the issue quickly and minimize any negative impact?

*Source: "Hello Stay Interviews, Goodbye Talent Loss: A Manager's Playbook" by Beverly Kaye and Sharon Jordan-Evans

Amplifying 1:1s

Set up a system to maximize your discussions so they are consistent and effective. Use this checklist to increase clarity and ensure accountability.

COMMUNICATING BEFORE A 1:1

- ◯ Schedule recurring meetings in the calendar
- ◯ Set expectations for their role and yours
- ◯ Create a shared agenda both can contribute to
- ◯ Send pre-questions or prompts in advance for more reflective thinkers

PREPARING FOR A 1:1

- ◯ Review notes from previous meetings to know where to follow up, celebrate, or provide feedback
- ◯ Ask others for feedback when necessary
- ◯ Practice tough conversations to build confidence

1:1 NOTE TAKING

- ◯ Handwrite notes in a notebook with tabs
- ◯ Record notes in a consistent capture tool
- ◯ Use a project management tool
- ◯ Maintain a specific page or document for each person
- ◯ Add dates to each meeting

1:1 MEETING REPEATABLES

- ◯ Reiterate the purpose of the discussion
- ◯ Start with an opening question
- ◯ Close with a thank you
- ◯ Ask for celebrations and wins
- ◯ Capture 'aha' moments or shifts

TRACKING ACCOUNTABILITY

- ◯ Set up a calendar reminder with milestones
- ◯ Track actions on a shared document
- ◯ Use a task management tool
- ◯ Add a recurring meeting to calendar
- ◯ Speak to an accountability partner

MAINTAINING PRESENCE

- ◯ Remove surrounding distractions
- ◯ Put phone on silent or focus mode
- ◯ Engage in a short grounding ritual
- ◯ Remove visible obstacles between you and the other person

Question Shifting

By shifting the questions we ask, we can uncover key facts, make decisions in uncertainty, or take action in times of change.

INSTEAD OF...	TRY...
"Do you have any questions?"	"What questions do you have?" "Where do you need clarification?"
"How are you?"	"What is the highlight of your day?" "On a scale of 1-5, how would you rate today? This week?"
"Where do you see yourself in 5 years?"	"What would you like to celebrate in 5 years' time?"
"What's wrong?"	"Is there something on your mind you'd like to share?"
"Do you need help?"	"What can I do to help?" "How can I be a resource to you?"
"What's the key to success?"	"What will you most need to succeed in the future?"
"What is the worst-case scenario?"	"What are all the scenarios you have thought of on this topic?"
"How do you deal with conflict?"	"What have you realized about yourself when faced with conflict?"

Source: Inspired by "A More Beautiful Question: The Power of Inquiry to Spark Breakthrough Ideas" by Warren Berger and "The Art of Powerful Questions: Catalyzing Insight, Innovation, and Action" by Eric E. Vogt, Juanita Brown, and David Isaacs

Question Shifting

INSTEAD OF...	TRY...
"Why do you think this happened?"	"What will you do now as a result of what has happened?"
"Where are you from?"	"How is where you grew up different from where you live now?"
"Why don't you agree with me?" "How can you not see it my way?"	"What would it take for us to be able to move forward?"
"What's going on?"	"How is your day shaping up so far?"
"Why didn't that work?"	"What would it take to make that work next time?"
"Great job!"	"Thanks for giving this project the time it deserved. I know you spent night and day getting it done."
"Good presentation!"	"Here are the things I really liked about your talk/presentation…"
"Anything else?"	"What are we missing?" "What am I missing?" "Is there anything additional you'd like to add or discuss?"

What now?

Keep this list close and catch yourself when you say something in the left column. Pause and quickly reframe with something from the right column.

Take A Field Trip

Field trips give your team fresh perspectives and lessons beyond typical leadership development. Choose experiences that match your goals and values. Use the list of ideas or brainstorm your own.

HISTORICAL SITES & MUSEUMS

Offers a window into the past to analyze historical decisions, dissect high-pressure situations, and reflect on long-term outcomes.

NATURE RETREATS

Invites leaders and teams into a neutral space that fosters personal growth, promotes reflection, reduces stress, and enhances focus.

TECH & START-UP HUBS

Opens the door to interact with entrepreneurs and be exposed to cutting-edge technologies and an entrepreneurial mindset.

CUSTOMER & CLIENT SITES

Empowers others to understand consumers' needs, challenges, and perspectives in order to improve decision-making and customer-centricity.

CULINARY EXPERIENCES

Facilitates lessons in creativity, teamwork, attention to detail, and the importance of quality, safety, and supply-chain management.

Chapter Reflection: Invest Your Time

Today's Date:

An insight or thought I've had this chapter is...

Where in your body did you feel this chapter the most?

A pattern I've noticed about myself is...

I want to talk with someone more about...

Capture an image or picture that best represents this chapter.

A song title for this chapter would be...

Foster Community

Words of Wonder

"Leadership is not about being in charge.
It's about taking care of those in your charge."
– Simon Sinek

"The greatness of a community is most accurately measured by the compassionate actions of its members."
– Coretta Scott King

"All leaders are incomplete; they need others to magnify their strengths and compensate for their weaknesses."
– "The Social Brain" by Robin Dunbar, Samantha Rockey, and Tracey Camilleri

Foster Community

What does this chapter cover?

Build and nurture meaningful connections, take on the roles necessary to meet the collective needs of your internal and external audience, and develop strategies to promote a more inclusive culture and community.

Why does this matter?

There is solid research supporting the idea that leaders who prioritize building meaningful connections, addressing collective needs, and fostering inclusive cultures positively impact team and organizational success.

What will you gain?

By addressing both internal and external needs, you will create a more engaged team, supportive culture, and will strengthen trust, inspire collaboration, and drive collective success.

EXERCISES

- Start A Conversation
- Sharing Matters
- Team Rituals
- Building Your Team
- The Words You Choose
- Mind Your Language
- Inclusive Leadership Audit
- Accountability
- Music Can Move You
- 12 Month Challenge

WRITING PROMPTS

- Defining Community
- Uniting with Purpose
- Unexpected Impact
- Check Your Bias
- Moment of Impact
- Letter to a Younger You

DEFINING COMMUNITY: What does "community" mean to you emotionally, physically, and mentally? What do you need to feel part of a community?

Date:

Start A Conversation

Use these prompts to spark meaningful dialogue within your internal and external communities. Leverage the responses to build stronger relationships, foster collaboration, and drive positive impact.

- Our community initiatives will be successful if/when…
- People feel most valued when…
- A mentor once taught me the importance of…
- My perception of our community shifted when…
- Ten years from now, I hope that our community will be known for…
- The next step to strengthen our connection is…
- What challenges me most is…
- In 2030, I hope people will look back and appreciate…
- What I know now that I didn't know a year ago is…
- When sharing ideas, it is important to keep in mind that…
- Those in our community are inspired by…
- The values of this community can best be described as…
- What energizes me most is…
- This community is important to me because…
- The last thing we should do is…

What now?

Select two or three sentence starters to introduce at the beginning of a meeting, and observe how the energy in the room shifts as people listen to one another.

Sharing Matters

Sharing personal stories fosters community by building authentic connections. Our unique experiences highlight our shared humanity and inspire deeper understanding. Capture a few ideas of the stories you are comfortable sharing.

What lesson did you learn growing up that you still carry with you?

I find it hard to...

When I was little...

My favorite thing to do is...

My biggest struggle has been...

My biggest success has been...

I hope that...

UNITING WITH PURPOSE: Reflect on a time you united a group with purpose. How did you ensure everyone felt valued and motivated? What impact did your efforts have?

Date:

Team Rituals

Ted Lasso, the soccer coach from the popular TV show, showed that team rituals help build connection, shared purpose, and mutual belief. His focus on believing in others' potential and turning challenges into opportunities for growth transformed both individual team members and the team as a whole.

Scan

Listen to Lasso Lessons: Ted on Life, Leadership & Learning

Cathy and Mike break down each episode of Ted Lasso with an eye towards what it can teach us about life, leadership, and learning.

TAKEAWAYS OR INSIGHTS

IDEAS FOR RITUALS

Building Your Team

Part of building a strong team and community is getting to know them. At your next in-person team event, ask a business partner to help you facilitate this exercise so that you can actively participate.

DIRECTIONS

Call out a color of the rainbow and present a corresponding slide with the color and question. Ask people to move into pairs or trios to discuss.

1 RED: What is one behavior or attitude in others that you find challenging to work with?

2 ORANGE: What truly motivates you to give your best at work?

3 YELLOW: What's the most creative or impactful idea you've ever contributed to a project?

4 GREEN: What is a fun or quirky purchase you've made that reflects your personality?

5 BLUE: What is one aspiration or goal you have for your future career?

6 INDIGO: What is the most daring professional risk you've ever taken, and what did you learn from it?

7 PURPLE: If you could make one significant change to your industry or organization, what would it be?

UNEXPECTED IMPACT: Has your choice of words or communication style ever had an unintended negative impact? What happened, and what did you learn?

Date:

The Words You Choose

Words have a profound impact. In difficult times, they can ease anxiety, build connections, shift perspectives, and shape how feedback or challenging conversations are received.

- The problem is…
- The issue is…
- The challenge is…
- Yes, but…
- I don't think…
- What concerns me is…
- We won't…
- You don't understand…
- I promise…

How might these phrases set the tone for a message?

- The opportunity here is…
- To solve this, we could…
- What we DO have is…
- One approach is to….
- What I can share is…
- What is in our reach is…
- A possibility to consider is…

How might shifting to these phrases change the tone of a message?

USE OFTEN

- I am grateful for…
- Let's celebrate…
- Thank you for…
- I hear you and value you.
- You make a difference.
- It's a difficult time and it makes sense that you feel how you do.

AVOID

- Do you know how lucky you are to have a job?
- I don't care how you do it, just do it.
- Don't be so emotional.
- I don't make the rules.
- I don't have time to explain myself.
- I'll just do it myself.

What Now?

Record yourself to see what words you choose in different situations. Shift where needed.

Mind Your Language

Our choice of words can shape an environment. Notice how the words on the left make you feel versus the more respectful alternatives on the right. Practice using these improved phrases to help everyone feel valued and included.

Avoid Potential Exclusion

"Hey guys"
"Disabled person"

"Hey team" or
"Hi, everyone"
"Person with a disability"

Maintain Neutral Professional Language

"That's a smart point."
"Sue, we haven't heard from you, what do you have to share?"
"What do you mean?"

"Your perspective is valuable."
"Let's hear from someone who hasn't spoken."
"Could you elaborate?"

Tone Considerations

"Wow, that's actually a good idea for you!"
"I'm wondering if maybe we could discuss..."
"I kind of think we might want to consider..."
"You totally messed this up."

"Would you like me to provide more context?"
"Thank you for sharing that perspective."
"Let's discuss the next action."
"I recommend we consider..."
"This needs some adjustment to..."

Pronouns and Identity

"Welcome, ladies and gentlemen."
"Where are you really from?"
"He'll be perfect for this leadership role."
"Her emotional response was over the top and inappropriate."

"Welcome, everyone."
"Tell me about your background..."
"This candidate has strong qualifications."
"The leader's communication could be better."

CHECK YOUR BIAS: Scan the QR code to take the Harvard Implicit Association Test (IAT). Reflect on the insights it provides and how they relate to your thoughts, behaviors, and decisions.

Date:

Inclusive Leadership Audit

Leaders who value diverse perspectives and create psychological safety, which ensures every team member feels respected, heard, and empowered, will reap the benefits of the unique talents on their team.

Take this Inclusive Leadership Audit to see how are you measuring up.

To establish psychological safety, I…	Weekly	Monthly	Never
□ Create opportunities for others to share diverse views			
□ Establish regular one-on-one check-ins			
□ Respond non-defensively to challenging feedback			
□ Acknowledge mistakes publicly and transparently			

To amplify voices, I…	Weekly	Monthly	Never
□ Actively listen without interrupting			
□ Highlight contributions from underrepresented colleagues			
□ Ensure equal speaking time in meetings			
□ Invite quiet team members to share their thoughts			

To mitigate bias, I…	Weekly	Monthly	Never
□ Regularly audit team decision-making processes			
□ Diversify hiring and promotion panels			
□ Challenge stereotypical assumptions			

To promote skill development, I…	Weekly	Monthly	Never
□ Create mentorship opportunities			
□ Develop the team's emotional intelligence			
□ Support workshops that advance expertise			

To ensure structural inclusion, I…	Weekly	Monthly	Never
□ Review policies for equitable language			
□ Accommodate flexible work arrangements			
□ Sponsor employee resource groups			
□ Establish clear anti-discrimination guidelines			

To continuously learn, I…	Weekly	Monthly	Never
□ Seek feedback on my leadership			
□ Maintain a personal reflection journal			
□ Stay informed about diversity and inclusion updates			

Accountability

Holding yourself accountable to your teams, stakeholders, and community as a leader involves intentional actions that build trust, demonstrate integrity, and create mutual respect.

DID YOU KNOW?

Research from the American Society of Training and Development (ASTD) found that your probability or likelihood of completing a goal looks like this:

	% likelihood of completing
Having an idea or goal.	10%
Consciously deciding that you will do it.	25%
Deciding when you will do it.	40%
Planning how to do it.	50%
Committing to someone that you will do it.	65%
Having a specific accountability appointment with someone you've committed to about it.	95%

I need to be held accountable for...

The person who can hold me accountable is...

MOMENT OF IMPACT: Write about a moment when you were mentored by someone and the impact that it had on you.

Date:

Music Can Move You

Creating emotional connection through music is a valuable tool for leaders to inspire, connect, and lead teams.

Part One:

Make a list of the songs that light you up, bring you calm, and provide you with a sense of confidence.

Part Two:

Start a themed playlist and ask your team to add their preferences to cultivate a rich tapestry of musical tastes and genres.

What now?

After your next team meeting or offsite, ask everyone to share a song title that represents their experience. As people share, take notes. Then create a playlist of everyone's songs and share it a few days after the offsite. It shows you were listening and will create a positive memory of the time together.

12-Month Community Challenge

This year-long challenge is a journey of connection, growth, and shared purpose. Commit to those that will inspire action and deepen bonds between you and your community.

- MONTH 1: Mentor a local entrepreneur
- MONTH 2: Host a community roundtable
- MONTH 3: Lead an industry meetup
- MONTH 4: Join a local advisory board
- MONTH 5: Create an internship program
- MONTH 6: Partner with a local startup
- MONTH 7: Have a student shadow you at work for a day
- MONTH 8: Judge a student competition
- MONTH 9: Support a local charity or arts program
- MONTH 10: Volunteer with your team
- MONTH 11: Share expertise at a library or school
- MONTH 12: Champion a local artist

LETTER TO A YOUNGER YOU: Imagine sitting down with your younger self at a pivotal age. What would you share about the importance of building community and giving back?

Date:

Chapter Reflection: Foster Community

Today's Date:

An insight or thought I've had this chapter is...

____

____

____

____

____

____

Where in your body did you feel this chapter the most?

A pattern I've noticed about myself is...

I want to talk with someone more about...

____

____

____

Capture an image or picture that best represents this chapter.

A song title for this chapter would be...

Tend to the Bigger Picture

Words of Wonder

“Big-picture thinking means looking beyond immediate results to the systems and structures that create lasting change.”
– Melinda French Gates

“If we don’t ask propelling questions of ourselves, someone is going to ask them of us, and by that time we will be behind the curve.”
– Adam Morgan and Mark Barden

“Someone’s sitting in the shade today because someone planted a tree a long time ago.”
– Warren Buffett

Tend to the Bigger Picture

What does this chapter cover?

Navigate the bigger picture while attending to the details. Evaluate what works and what could be better as you consider long-term and large-scale projects. This chapter may benefit from collaboration with fellow leaders when making informed and strategic decisions.

Why does this matter?

By making intentional decisions and addressing what needs improvement, you will build trust, inspire progress, and ensure your vision becomes reality in a way that serves the collective good.

What will you gain?

Sustained growth, financial success, increased engagement, and the ability to adapt to challenges and opportunities with confidence and clarity.

EXERCISES

- Crafting Precise Goals
- Trend Spotting
- Alternative Futures
- Business Continuity
- Build Your Bench
- Succession Template
- Know Your Numbers
- Risk Appetite
- The 5 E Decision Path
- 8-Ball Decision-Making
- Observe and Review
- Leave A Mark

WRITING PROMPTS

- Goal Clarity
- Navigation Plan
- Leave it to Succeed It
- Strategic Balance
- Letter to Future Self
- In Five Years
- Leadership Lookback

Crafting Precise Goals

The way you articulate a goal determines its potential for success. The art of goal-setting begins with a single, critical verb and a precisely constructed statement that cuts through ambiguity and provides immediate clarity. The verb you choose is powerful and could be the difference between a goal that inspires action or one that dissolves due to vagueness.

Use this verb list as a guide when setting goals for yourself or your team.

REMEMBER

Define, Describe, Label, List, Match, Name, Outline, Recall, Repeat, Replicate, Select, State

UNDERSTAND

Classify, Convert, Describe, Explain, Identify, Indicate, Map, Predict, Rewrite, Translate, Summarize

APPLY

Change, Compute, Demonstrate, Dramatize, Illustrate, Modify, Operate, Practice, Predict, Produce, Solve

ANALYZE

Calculate, Categorize, Compare, Diagram, Differentiate, Distinguish, Illustrate, Model, Question, Separate, Test

EVALUATE

Appraise, Assess, Coordinate, Defend, Estimate, Measure, Rank, Rate, Recommend, Select, Test

CREATE

Arrange, Assemble, Compose, Construct, Design, Develop, Generate, Prepare, Revise, Synthesize, Write

Examples

Poor: Build and deploy a marketing strategy by the end of Q2.
Good: Build out a marketing strategy that can be deployed by the end of Q2.

Poor: Take the lead as the expert in AI.
Good: Become a recognized thought leader in AI by the end of the year.

GOAL CLARITY: Write your goals for the next quarter. Once written, highlight the verbs. If there is more than one verb in a sentence, then you have more than one goal in the sentence. Rewrite your goal with one verb for clarity and specificity.

Date:

EXAMPLE OF MORE THAN ONE GOAL IN A SENTENCE

Develop and increase product portfolio offerings to improve sales.

EXAMPLE OF A REWRITE WITH ONE SPECIFIC GOAL

Drive a 10% increase in sales by expanding the product portfolio with two new offerings this quarter.

Trend Spotting

Thinking critically about trends, their potential impacts, and actions to stay ahead of changes in your industry allows you to navigate complexity, capitalize on opportunities, and lead your organization in an ever-changing world.

LIST THE TOP 5 TRENDS CURRENTLY SHAPING YOUR INDUSTRY OR AREA OF INTEREST.	IS IT AN OPPORTUNITY, AN UNKNOWN OR A RISK? (SELECT ALL THAT APPLY)	WHAT PROACTIVE ACTION CAN YOU TAKE BASED ON YOUR ASSESSMENT?
Example Shift toward subscription-based models	✓ ✓	Adapt content to local tastes and cultures.

What now?

Map out a 30-day action plan to explore, leverage, or prepare for this trend. Engage contributors that will add value to the project.

Alternative Futures

By exploring alternative futures, you can anticipate challenges, prompt innovation, mitigate risks, and develop adaptive strategies to enable proactive decision-making in a complex and unpredictable landscape.

Individually or with your team, think about a future decision, project, or initiative and capture your responses to each world below.

1 World One: A Thriving Future
What decisions led to this thriving future?

2 World Two: A Challenging Future
What were the mistakes or missed opportunities?

3 World Three: An Unexpected Turn
What surprised you most? What didn't you see coming?

What now?

Invite your team to discuss these worlds and what's practical to adopt or adapt.

NAVIGATION PLAN: Write a letter to your team describing how you would navigate a major challenge your organization might face. Add the strategies, mindset, and actions you would take to guide them.

Date:

Business Continuity

Check off the items you already have in place as you evaluate your existing Business Continuity Plan (BCP) or create one for the future. This whole-brain checklist based on the Emergenetics® framework will help you assess whether your plan is ready to support you during a major business crisis or natural disaster.

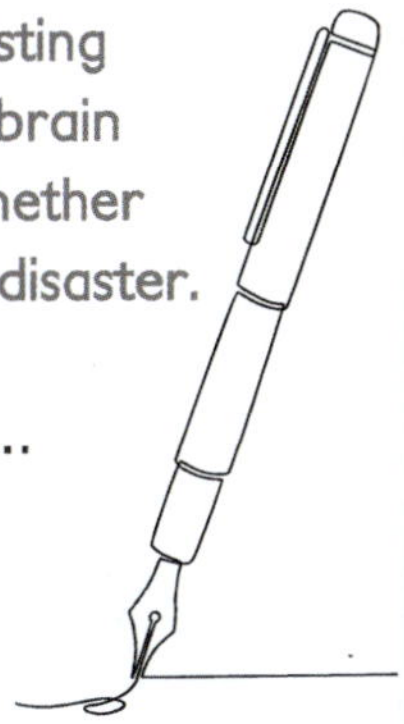

THOSE WITH AN ANALYTICAL THINKING PREFERENCE NEED YOU TO…

- ☐ Outline your goals and objectives for the Business Continuity Plan
- ☐ Share the financial impact or potential loss of anticipated shifts
- ☐ List critical business functions required for continuity
- ☐ Define your metrics for success

THOSE WITH A STRUCTURAL THINKING PREFERENCE NEED YOU TO…

- ☐ Share the legal and compliance impact of the situation
- ☐ Create detailed scenarios for each potential crisis/scenario
- ☐ Identify and list all resources needed to keep critical functions afloat
- ☐ Outline explicit steps in your response strategy for each scenario

THOSE WITH A CONCEPTUAL THINKING PREFERENCE NEED YOU TO…

- ☐ Describe the reputational risk of the situation
- ☐ Share the vision of success after responding to the crisis scenario
- ☐ Identify potential long-term threats to the organization
- ☐ Provide high-level recovery strategies that address future needs beyond your immediate response

THOSE WITH A SOCIAL THINKING PREFERENCE NEED YOU TO…

- ☐ Share stakeholder impact, employee safety, and community needs
- ☐ Identify a task force who will lead the response with compassion
- ☐ Highlight the specific teams and departments described in the response plan
- ☐ Convey the importance of supporting each stakeholder group

PEOPLE MIGHT BEHAVE OR RESPOND DIFFERENTLY, SO YOU MAY NEED TO…

- ☐ Identify multiple two-way approaches or platforms for communications
- ☐ Share visuals, charts, and graphs to allow others to digest a strategy
- ☐ Create a timeline of specific milestones and targets
- ☐ Define absolute requirements (e.g., regulatory or compliance)

What now?

Ensure the work behind each item is completed or delegated so your Business Continuity Plan is ready for activation when needed.

LEAVE IT TO SUCCEED IT: If you were to resign or take a leave of absence, how well-prepared is your team to succeed without your guidance? What can you do to ensure they continue to thrive in your absence?

Date:

Build Your Bench

Building your leadership bench is an ongoing effort that ensures a smooth transition when senior roles become vacant. Whether due to resignations, retirements, or unexpected events, having a prepared successor is key. Planning shouldn't start upon an exit - developing and mentoring potential leaders can take years. To secure the strategies and knowledge transfer needed for a successful future transition, the time to start is now.

Use these notes and the template on the next page to begin to think about your succession plan.

READINESS LEVELS DEFINED

Ready now: Someone who has 90% of the competency & experience to take the role now
Ready in 12 months: Shorter-term candidate who needs additional responsibility & exposure
Ready in 24 months: Medium-term candidate who requires additional responsibility & skills
Ready in 36 months: Longer-term candidate who requires significant development
Interim coverage: Able to provide coverage on an interim basis (~6 months)
On the radar: New to role or business with potential or additional time required to assess
Not a fit for the future: Person does not want a role or is not a fit a fit for the future

EXAMPLES OF COMPETENCIES, SKILLS, & CAPABILITIES

- Business insight
- Develops talent
- Financial acumen
- Resourceful
- Strategic mindset
- Drives vision and purpose
- Communicates effectively
- Interpersonal savvy
- Customer-centric
- Analytical mindset
- Demonstrates self-awareness
- Situational adaptability
- Instills trust
- Attention to details
- Global perspective
- Builds strong networks
- Tech-savvy
- Cultivates innovation

EXAMPLES OF POTENTIAL DERAILERS

- Struggles to adapt to change or new challenges
- Overlooks cultural nuances
- Creates confusion when sharing goals
- Overconfident
- Self-doubting
- Closed off to support, coaching, or feedback
- Over-reliance on an advocate or mentor
- Does not assume accountability
- Avoids difficult conversations

GROWTH OPPORTUNITIES

- Gain 360 feedback
- Lead a high impact project
- Take on an international assignment or secondment
- Work with a mentor or coach
- Speak at a conference
- Attend a networking event
- Take part in senior meetings
- Pursue advanced education

Succession Template

PERSON'S NAME

CURRENT ROLE

YEARS IN ROLE

RETENTION LIKELIHOOD

HIGH MED LOW

READINESS LEVEL

- ☐ Ready now
- ☐ Ready in 12 months
- ☐ Ready in 24 months
- ☐ Ready in 36 months
- ☐ Interim Coverage
- ☐ On the radar
- ☐ Not a fit for future

CURRENT COMPETENCIES

COMPETENCIES TO DEVELOP

POTENTIAL DERAILERS

AREAS TO STRENGTHEN

- ☐ Commercial mindset
- ☐ Industry knowledge
- ☐ Communication skills
- ☐ Position-specific expertise
- ☐ Management skills
- ☐ Interpersonal skills
- ☐ Leadership skills

GROWTH OPPORTUNITIES

STRATEGIC BALANCE: How do you navigate the tension between creative thinking and analytical decision-making when shaping a strategy? Which do you lean on more, and why?

Date:

Know Your Numbers

Knowing your numbers will provide you with the foundation for informed decision-making, accountability, and strategic planning, and allow you to lead with confidence by bridging the gap between vision and reality.

Take the quiz to test your current knowledge of your numbers.

1 What was last month's revenue?

a) I know this! It was ________

b) My best guess is ________

c) I have no idea

2 How many people are currently on my team?

a) My team has exactly ______ people

b) I would need to ask someone

c) I don't keep track of those details

3 What was the net cash flow for the organization last month?

a) It was ___________ exactly

b) Somewhere in the __________ range

c) I have not looked into it

4 What is the current profit margin percentage, and has it changed over the past year?

a) ____% and it went [up or down]

b) I would need to look at some numbers

c) I have a team for that

5 What was the employee turnover rate for the last year?

a)_______ % give or take

b) Need to call HR or People Team

c) My team stayed intact

6 What is your current Net Promoter Score (NPS)?

a) Last time I checked it was _______

b) I think it is high

c) We have never looked into that

7 Which product or service generated the highest profit last quarter?

a) ___________ was the most profitable

b) Let me ask my team lead

c) I don't know

8 What percentage of your projects are completed within the planned budget and timeline?

a) _____%

b) I would have to ask the team

c) None of them

9 What was the Return on Investment (ROI) for the most recent project?

a) _____% [above or below]

b) I will get back to you tomorrow

c) Ask the finance team

10 As it stands today, are we on track to a positive net-profit for this year?

a) Yes, I am sure of it

b) Not my top concern

c) I really hope so

Know Your Numbers

After completing the quiz, tally up your total number of 'a' answers to calculate your score. Identify which metrics you need to sharpen so that you feel prepared to discuss them confidently at any given moment.

Calculate Your Score

(Tally all 'a' answers)

/10

Scorecard

8-10 = You seem to know your numbers
5-7 = You might be getting by
0-4 = You have work to do

Analyze Current Performance

Write down the specific and current value for each metric to correspond with the previous page.

1 Last month revenue

2 # of people on team

3 Last month net cash

4 Profit margin %

5 Employee turnover

6 Current NPS #

7 Highest Profit Product/service

8 % completed on time and on budget

9 Recent project ROI

10 YTD net profit

Future-Proof Your Numbers

Set goals for each metric and develop a strategy to achieve them if not there yet. E.g., reduce costs, boost customer retention, etc.

1 Last month revenue

2 # of people on team

3 Last month net cash

4 Profit margin %

5 Employee turnover

6 Current NPS #

7 Highest Profit Product/service

8 % completed on time and on budget

9 Recent project ROI

10 YTD net profit

Risk Appetite

Knowing the damaging events or perceived risks that could impact your business helps you make strategic decisions, navigate challenges, and potentially seize opportunities. Move through the next two pages to examine your risk appetite.

1

When it comes to your business, what do you value?

E.g., profits, reputation, sales, employee retention

2

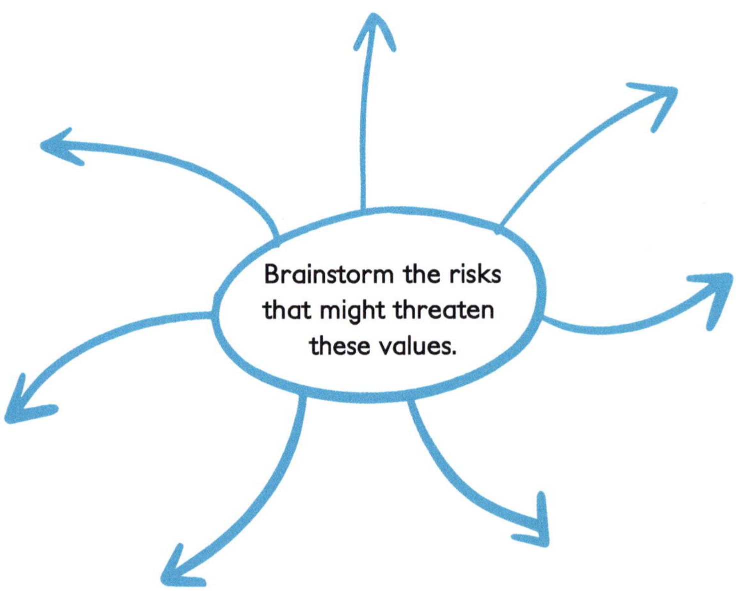

3

Draw a circle around the things you captured above that you want to do something about. These are usually the ones that would cause the most pain if they happened or are more likely to occur.

Source: Uyen Vo, Risk Expert and Facilitator

Risk Appetite

4 Place your circled items in this table. For each one, identify the likelihood of it happening, the impact if it did, and actions to reduce negative effects.

RISK Those you circled	LIKELIHOOD High - Med - Low	IMPACT	RESPONSE
Example Reputation	M	• Financial • Slammed in press. • Client won't work with us again.	• Assemble a crisis communication team. • Develop an authentic, transparent response.

5 Because things are always changing, what reminders can you set in place to review this regularly with your team and stakeholders?

What now?

Schedule a meeting with relevant stakeholders to review and discuss what high risk items you have identified in this exercise.

The 5 E Decision Path

The 5 E Decision Path is a framework to help you work through complex decisions. Choose a situation that needs resolution and work through each 'E' to develop a practical solution that can be implemented upon completing this exercise.

MY SITUATION

Explore – Spark Possibilities

List all options, including big, small, unconventional, and "what if" ideas, without judgment.

Elect – Make Your Choice

Weigh the pros and cons of each option. Ask yourself which option will make the biggest positive impact.

The 5 E Decision Path

Explain - Articulate the Plan

Communicate your plan in a way that connects with everyone involved. Share the "why" and the details.

Execute - Take Action

Keep your team involved by assigning roles, setting milestones, and creating a rhythm for tracking progress.

Evaluate - Reflect & Improve

After completion, review the results with an open mind. Invite feedback to see what could be refined for the future.

What now?

Choose a new situation and work through the Es again. Use lessons learned and make any adjustments to this process that you find helpful.

8-Ball Decision-Making

When a simple "Yes" or "No" won't suffice,
consider the 8-Ball answer that best fits your situation.

Affirmative

It is certain

Yes – definitely

Most likely

Signs point to yes

Non-committal

Reply hazy, try again

Ask again later

Better not tell you now

Cannot predict now

Concentrate & ask again

Negative

My reply is no

My sources say no

Outlook not so good

Very doubtful

EXERCISE:

Say your question out loud.
Use your intuition to determine which 8-Ball response resonates most.

What else might you need in order to be certain about your decision?

For example, do you need to...

- Identify specific risks
- Develop contingency strategies
- Weigh opportunities and drawbacks
- Gain diverse perspectives
- Prepare a brief to outline your decision
- Schedule consultation meetings
- Synthesize team input
- Identify information gaps
- Set specific timelines
- List out evidence supporting your intuition
- Cross-reference gut feeling with available data
- Deconstruct challenges into smaller components
- Create an action plan

What is your next immediate action?

What now?

After selecting your response, write a one-paragraph explanation of your reasoning, potential risks, and next action.

LETTER TO FUTURE SELF: Write a letter to your future self. Include bold moves you have made, fears you have overcome, answers to the questions you would want to know in 6-12 months, what you have learned, and anything else that comes to mind.

Date:

Observe and Review

Select a leader in the news and write a review analyzing their leadership qualities, much like an art critic would. Focus on elements like body language, expressions, words, gestures, tone, pace, and how these contribute to their leadership image.

The leader I am reviewing is...

In a nutshell, I would describe their leadership image or style as...

The qualities they exhibit are...

-
-
-
-
-
-

Did you Know...

A Wondershift study found that the most desired traits in a leader are the ability to "empower" and "show empathy."

Areas they may face challenges are...

The lasting impression they are making in their field, organization, or society is...

IN FIVE YEARS: Imagine your organization five years from now. What role will your leadership play in getting it there? What needs to happen today to make that vision a reality?

Date:

Leave A Mark

Take a moment to reflect on the impact you want to have on your teams, your organization, and your community.

> "Let your life be like a snowflake, leave a mark but not a stain." - Grandma

What impact do you want to have?

How do you want to be remembered?

What positive changes do you want to bring about?

LEADERSHIP LOOKBACK: When people look back on you and your leadership, what do you hope they will say about you?

Date:

Chapter Reflection: Tend to the Bigger Picture

Today's Date:

An insight or thought I've had this chapter is…

____

____

____

____

____

____

Where in your body did you feel this chapter the most?

A pattern I've noticed about myself is…

Capture an image or picture that best represents this chapter.

I want to talk with someone more about…

____

____

____

A song title for this chapter would be…

A Moment for Reflection

Reflection Wrap Up

ACHIEVEMENTS

What are the top three leadership achievements you feel most proud of?

KEY LEARNINGS

What did you learn about yourself based on the exercises you completed?

GROWTH INSIGHTS

Where would you like to improve this year?

MOMENTUM

Who can you partner with to celebrate your successes and hold you accountable?

COMMITMENT

What will you make the time to commit to going forward?

Appendix

Sources & References

2 Quote | Aristotle, Greek Philosopher
Quote | Judy Goldberg, Founder and Leadership Expert

3 Data | Insight, Tasha Eurich, Author

27 Framework | Emergenetics® International

30 Quote | Martin Luther King Jr., Civil Rights Leader, Activist and Political Philosopher
Quote | Maya Angelou, Civil Rights Activist and Poet
Quote | Tony Gaskins, Motivational Speaker, Author, and Coach

31 Data | Daniel Goleman, Author

36 Leadership Philosophy | Colin Powell, Former United States Secretary of State

54 Quote | Jonathan Estrin, Television Producer and Writer, Director
Quote | Robin Sharma, Writer

56 Data | Phil Dobson, Author and Founder of BrainWorkshops

58 Theory | George Leonard, Founder Human Potential Movement

61 Speech | "Great Leadership is a Network, Not a Hierarchy," Gitte Frederiksen

63 Podcast | Armored Versus Daring Leadership, Dr. Brené Brown

66 Study | Gartner and Capital Analytics, Sun Microsystems 2007
Study | Moving Ahead and Deloitte, 2024

69 Study | Wake Up and Wondershift, 2023

71 Book | Hello Stay Interviews, Goodbye Talent Loss, Beverly Kaye and Sharon Jordan-Evans

73 Book | A More Beautiful Question, Warren Berger
Book | The Art of Powerful Questions, Eric E. Vogt, Juanita Brown, and David Isaacs

78 Quote | Simon Sinek, Author and Speaker
Quote | Coretta Scott King, Author, Activist, and Civil Rights Leader
Quote | The Social Brain, Robin Dunbar, Samantha Rockey, and Tracey Camilleri

84 Podcast | Ted Lasso, Lasso Lessons: Ted on Life, Leadership & Learning

89 Project Implicit | Harvard Implicit Association Test

91 Research | American Society of Training and Development (ASTD)

98 Quote | Melinda French Gates, Philanthropist, Businesses Woman, and Global Advocate
Quote | Adam Morgan and Mark Barden, Storytellers and Authors
Quote | Warren Buffett, Investor and Philanthropist

105 Theory | Business Continuity Plan (BCP) based on Emergenetics® Framework

112 Framework | Uyen Vo, Risk Expert and Facilitator

120 Quote | Grandma, Entrepreneur and Maker of the best homemade apple sauce

Words from Wondershift Leaders

"This journal is fresh, clear, and engaging. The questioning prompts and exercises offer the right balance of depth and simplicity. It's a leadership tool that speaks to modern, open-minded professionals looking to elevate their impact."
Quinn, Team Lead, Healthcare

"The design may be colorful and playful, but don't let that fool you. The exercises are relevant and crafted to spark deep reflection and important conversations that drive growth."
Arno, COO, Technology

"The content was spot on and your energy and delivery were excellent. I received unsolicited feedback that it was extremely valuable. It provoked new ways of thinking for our team that I know will deliver results."
Dave, VP, Commercial, Sustainable Packaging

"This book challenges you to pause and reflect, urging you to re-examine, refine, or even let go of your preconceived notions. It's a serious, transformative resource for leaders committed to growth."
Ruth, SVP Marketing
Media

Thank You

A special thanks to...

Madeline Arnoldy for her exceptional partnership in bringing this second book to fruition. Her ability to maintain project momentum, challenge existing perspectives, introduce innovative thinking, and meticulously manage details was instrumental in elevating the work beyond our original vision.

Jilleen Livingston for her invaluable contributions to the leadership research study mentioned throughout. When in her final year at the Stern School of Business, New York University, pursuing a Master of Arts in Industrial and Organizational Psychology, Jilleen brought structure, insights, and a deep understanding of both quantitative and qualitative research methodologies. Her ability to lead interviews, and review the data to translate how these findings could address real workplace challenges made a lasting impact on the research and practicality of this work.

My exceptional editorial team, Alexandra Resich, Meredith Conte, Sophie Clark, and Susan Goldberg who devoted countless hours to scrutinize every page, challenge my prose, verify sources, and ensure the highest quality of this work. Their keen insights and unwavering commitment transformed this journal.

My clients, family, and friends who continue to champion me in each project I take on. I am deeply grateful for your encouragement, unwavering support, and love, which make every challenge more rewarding and every success more meaningful.

About Judy Goldberg

Judy Goldberg is the founder of Wondershift LLC. She collaborates with leaders around the globe to elevate their leadership capabilities, define strategy, design organizations, and maximize the collective intelligence in a room. With nearly 30 years of experience, Judy transforms how leaders think, behave, and work. She uses her expertise to help leaders expand their awareness and uncover innovative solutions.

Judy designs and facilitates experiential leadership development programs, strategy sessions, and events that cut through noise, fostering meaningful breakthroughs. She elevates communication, collaboration, and productivity within teams using insights from neuroscience.

A seasoned global speaker and consultant, Judy has delivered keynotes and moderated panels worldwide. She brings a global perspective, a commercial and strategic mindset, and a focus on the shift: Where are you now? Where do you want to be? And how do you get there?

Judy's career journey is a testament to adaptability and growth. She built the International Learning & Development function for Discovery Channel, was one of the first Training & Development Officers for Royal Caribbean Cruise Lines, and holds an undergrad degree in Education and a Master of Arts in Educational Leadership.

After 10 years in London, Judy is now based in New York City. She continues to travel, nurture her passion for street art, ride her Peloton, spend time with her nieces and nephews, and work closely with local nonprofits.

Notes

Notes

Notes

Wonder no more...

WONDERSHIFT

Printed in Great Britain
by Amazon

63083120R00087